# AFRICAN DEVELOPMENTS IN THE DOLDRUMS

Henry Augustine Brown-Acquaye

authorHOUSE®

*AuthorHouse*™
*1663 Liberty Drive, Suite 200*
*Bloomington, IN 47403*
*www.authorhouse.com*
*Phone: 1-800-839-8640*

*First published by AuthorHouse 3/25/2008*

*ISBN: 978-1-4343-7305-2 (sc)*

*Library of Congress Control Number: 2008902244*

*Printed in the United States of America*
*Bloomington, Indiana*

*This book is printed on acid-free paper.*

This book is dedicated to members of my family:
Julie, Maame Adwoa, Papa Kodwo and Kweku Annan
and also to all concerned about the dilemma facing African
countries in their socio-economic developments

# ACKNOWLEDGEMENT

This book owes its presence more to others than to the author. The political thoughts and concerns for the development of the African continent of many African scholars and leaders were the catalysts for the efforts by the author to undertake writing such a book. .Not being an economist, a lawyer or development specialist, but an inorganic chemistry lecturer, the abysmal living conditions in most African countries cannot be overlooked by an African trained scientist like the author. The purpose for the book has been to bring to the fore some personal thoughts and concerns with respect to the economic and social developments in these developing countries. Such an enterprise could not have taken roots without the great contributions of African scholars through their academic publications  and contributions at international conferences. These African scholars received intellectual support from internationally recognized academics whose views have been widely published in books and journals.

My greatest appreciation goes to Professor Bill Cobern, the Director of the Mallinson Institute for Science Education at the Western Michigan University,Kalamazoo, Michigan State who was my research associate during my six months period there at the university as a Fulbright Visiting Scholar. His works and writings on Worldview theory and Science Education Research greatly guided my thinking and writings.

Special thanks go to the Fulbright Commission of the USA Department of State for the award o f a fellowship to enable me go to the Western Michigan University to do research on Multicultural Science versus Universal Science

Mention must also be made of the efforts of the staff of Colleagues International, Michigan Chapter, in particular Ms Diane Downing, in making my six months stay at Kalamazoo culturally welcome and educative

# CONTENTS

# INTRODUCTION

The African Union a grouping of fifty-three (53) independent African States with a total population (2006) of eight hundred and fifty million (850million) people. Most of these states especially those in sub-Sahara Africa keep on attracting international focus because of the deplorable living conditions of their citizens. In most of these states it is very common to find an expectant mother to lose her life and that of the new-born baby while delivering the baby. No health facilities are available for the expectant mother. Even where there are some health facilities as there may  be no trained nurses or midwives, no potable water, no lean baby napkins, no electricity, no drugs and nothing worthy to be associated with health delivery system. These conditions lead to very high maternal and infant mortalities. The situation is worsened by the fact that the sub-Sahara African region is the most affected  area in the world with respect to the rapid spread of the HIV and the AIDS pandemic. Thus the very little health facilities available are stretched to their limits due to the HIV/AIDS problems.

Abject poverty is evident in the faces of the children and their parents. Poor sanitation, poor housing, poor road networks, over utilized agricultural farmlands and desperation for survival by the citizens are daily issues which the governments have to handle. Provision of basic education for the children is not high on the government's agenda when the issue of provision of food is taking all the attention. Learning and teaching materials are not available and so is the lack of trained teachers.

These myriads of problems push the governments to adopt ad-hoc solutions which do not help in the development of the communities. Long term serious planning is not resorted to as the extent of the poverty, of the prevailing communicable but preventable diseases, t of environmental degradation call for immediate action on daily basis to alleviate the problems which overwhelm the authorities.

There is abundant offer of external assistance in the form of economic aid, human resources, health and educational inputs from foreign governments, international non-governmental organizations (NGOS), various agencies of the United Nations, bilateral donor agencies and overseas philanthropic organizations to these developing countries. The impact of all these assistances are not strong on the lives of the ordinary citizens. The situation is further exacerbated by ethic and tribal conflicts in the communities which then divert and occupy the attention of governments.

The situation in these sub-Sahara African developing countries is grave and needs the inputs from the 'global village' to pull them from their unacceptable living conditions

The failure or reluctance of the western industralised countries to come to the assistance of the developing countries with very drastic and innovative measures will push these developing countries into the open and welcoming hands of China which will lead to a change in the dynamics of international world power.

It must be realized that in the present state of the world, science and technology pervades all aspects of living. Recognition of this situation must therefore be the dynamo to invest heavily in science and technology education. The practical applications of science and technology create the environment for the eradication of preventable diseases, alleviation of poverty, improvement in health facilities and sanitation, and in housing facilities. Governments in these developing countries cannot afford to disregard research in the basic and applied sciences as major factors to the long-term social and economic developments. Capable students in the sciences in these countries should be identified and nurtured and encouraged. Specific actions for strengthening science and technology capacities must be initiated in addition to the recognition of the vital roles of the universities. For science and technology education to be meaningful, effective planning and management cannot be ruled out.

The question of the brain drain should not be used as excuses for the non-provision of realistic funds for science and technology. Looked at from another angle, the brain drain could be considered as a kind of a process that can contribute to the creation and transfer of knowledge.

In this era of globalization, one cannot rule out the emergence of a mass of skilled workforce from the developing countries to the western industrialized countries. It is a welcome situation which can be exploited to the benefit of the developing countries. The need for the developing countries to engage in good governance through democratic practices necessitates 'openness' in all spheres of government. Openness and globalization can be taken as antidotes to underdevelopment and poverty and also considered as prime factors for accelerated improvement in the poor  living conditions in the countries.

Improved agricultural practices have to be intensified if these developing countries are to be self-sufficient in food production and food security. The book is structured in such a way as to make each of the chapters thorough and comprehensive.

Chapter One deals with the constructivist theory of learning which has its roots in the western worldview. This theory is however being used and is incorporated in the teaching and learning processes in the developing countries without due cognition of the cultural milieu on the students in these countries. The western worldview and the Ghanaian worldviews are separately discussed and hurdles and supports for the constructivist theory are highlighted.

Chapter Two looks at the model of science and technology for development in the developing countries which have been heralded to solve the problems of underdevelopment in these countries. Although the practice of science and technology have been found very effective in the western industrialized countries for their social and economic developments such a scenario cannot be identified in the developing countries. The failure of this model in Ghana is taken as a case study.

Chapter Three considers the whole gamut of what constitutes globalization, science and technology education in the developing countries and prevailing conditions that qualify some countries to be designated as 'developing'.

Chapter Four discusses the problems faced by the governments of the continent with respect to the search to establish a n African Union Government. The genesis of the Organization for African Unity, the problems encountered and its metamorphosis to the African Union re discussed .It is finally recognized that it is only through a Continental African Government that the intractable problems of the continent with regards to socio-economic development can be effectively put under control.

There is the Postlude which summarizes most of the ideas and makes some suggestions.

Henry A. Brown-Acquaye
Pedu, Cape Coast

# CHAPTER ONE:

# CONSTRUCTIVISM AND THE GHANAIAN WORLDVIEW

## INTRODUCTION

The pressing desires of the government to alleviate poverty, eradicate diseases, hunger and to improve on the living conditions of its citizens have made it imperative for the development of scientific and technological skills among Ghanaian students.

For most governments in the developing countries, science and technology are the ways for the future. Yoweri Museveni, President of Uganda has noted that for Africa to exert itself globally, it would need to have a critical mass of educated population that will have the capacity to utilize technology in order to transform the natural resources to wealth (Museveni,1995). It is therefore unfortunate that regardless of all the efforts put into science and technology education the results in economic development, industrialization, health provision and general raising of the living conditions of the citizens have not been encouraging in most developing countries in Africa. Poverty, preventable diseases, poor sanitation, poor health facilities, poor housing, poor transport and communication systems are still very visible in these countries, years after gaining political independence from their colonial masters.

The worldviews of the western colonial administrators differ significantly from the worldviews of the colonized countries. Using the constructivist theory of learning which has its basis in the western worldview, in the teaching of science in the Ghanaian environment, is bound to face difficulties. Placing science in context is very important in the constructivist theory of learning. The different worldviews need to be scrutinized to find areas which can be put together to facilitate the teaching and learning processes in the developing countries.

## SUB-CULTURES

It is now well documented that science is a sub-culture of western or Euro-American culture.(Dart,1972, Jegede,1995,Maddock,19 81,Ogawa,1986).As part of the culture, western scientists possess a well –defined system of norms, values, beliefs, expectations, some of which may be very different from the values, norms and beliefs of the Ghanaian science students. In a non-western developing country, educators generally consider science to be a second culture and foreign for the students in contrast to their own traditional and cherished culture.

In his inaugural lecture, titled "Race, Culture, Evolution and Traditional Worldviews: Challenges for Science Education", delivered at the University of the Western Cape, Bellville, South Africa,on September 22,1995, Ogunniyi stated 'In reference to education in general and science education, in particular, it is important to recognize the varied worldviews that students bring to the learning situation and their potential to enhance or hinder the acquisition of scientific knowledge or skills… Although theoretically, the tenets of science may be universal, the way in which they are conceived, applied and communicated is not necessarily so. Also, the value system prevalent in the culture of the students to a large extent, determines their focused attention. In Africa at least, the success or otherwise of science instruction ultimately depends on our understanding of where the students are coming from and to take them from thence...My personal experiences as a child, a student and later as a teacher and researcher convince me well enough that as far as science education is concerned, not much can be achieved as long as the learner's cultural background or cosmology is relegated to the background...His view of the universe was quite distinct from that presented to him in science classes....I was reared in the Yoruba culture with its rich anthropomorphic world view. My contact with the physical universe and the study of that universe were influenced by a dynamic culturally organized macro-thought of metaphysics, the world of gods, goddesses, spirits, divinities, natural forces, titularly deities, ancestors, taboos, witch, emeres-children with powers of reincarnations, magic, mysticisms and of course indigenous science and technology. Therefore, my first encounter with the study of nature started before my first day at school. But it was a different approach...science, empiricism, metaphysics were all part of my upbringing.' (Ogunniyi,1995)

From a cultural perspective, Ghanaian students have a very different knowledge of the natural world from that held by the western scientist. While the western scientist aims to gain knowledge of the natural world for the sake of knowledge and for power over nature and other people(Peat,1994), the Ghanaians aim to acquire knowledge for survival and to live peacefully and harmoniously with nature. They accept the mystery of nature while the western scientist attempts to explain the mystery of nature. The Ghanaian student therefore comes to the classroom with culturally validated ideas about the world. It is therefore not the school which is the principal formative agent for them.

The existence of different cultures between which the Ghanaian science student commutes, calls for realistic approach to the teaching of western science in order not to cause alienation. The commuting is a sort of border crossing and students should be helped to develop the facility to cross these borders from the everyday subcultures of their peers, family and tribe into the subcultures of school science, and science and technology.(Aikenhead,1997)

From observation, school science in Ghana is western-based. Its goal is thus to transmit both the sub-culture of science and the dominant western culture(Archibald,1995, Krughy and Smoska, 1995, Stanley and Brickhouse, 1994).The transmission of a scientific sub-culture can either be supportive or disruptive to students.(Contreras and Lee,1990).If the sub-culture of science fits harmoniously with the everyday culture of the students, enculturation would ensue and this would be in support of the science instruction. On the other hand, if the students' worldview is not in tune with the sub-culture of science and the students are coerced to abandon or marginalize their own indigenous way of knowing or have it substituted with a new way of knowing, there would be great destruction and would result in assimilation (Jegede,1995, Maclvor.1995). Most students in Ghana will not easily accept assimilation. Their efforts will be to contain the situation by resorting to strategies that would enable them to pass their science courses without learning the content expected of them by their teachers and society. This is an easy way out, since in practice most schooling is based on the ability to answer questions unrelated to any context outside of the school room.(Latour,1987) The most desirable situation is the one where the student can learn the western science without being harmfully assimilated by the dominant western culture. Enculturation also cannot be envisaged,as the Ghanaian culture and the western science culture do not synchronize in a lot of areas. In Africa generally, students' traditional cosmologies conflict with the norms, values, beliefs expectations and conventional actions of the western science community.(Jegede and Okebukola,1991)

The ability of the Ghanaian student to move into the western science depends greatly on how similar or dissimilar the two worldviews are. Four types of transitions can be envisaged

1. Smooth transitions, which occur when the two worldviews are congruent;
2. Manageable transitions for different worldviews
3. Hazardous transitions fore diverse worldviews; and
4. Impossible transitions for highly discordant worldviews.(Phelan,1991)

Successful border crossing would enhance students' capability to 'raid western science for practical ends and achieve desired goals' (Aikenhead,1996, Layton et al,1993.)

The Japanese technological success in the 20th. Century was driven by the fact that" the Japanese never lost their cultural identity when introducing western science and technology. They introduced only the practical products of western science and technology, never its epistemology or worldviews."(Ogunniyi et al. 1995).The Japanese experience fits in well with Spinder's Acculturation which is described as a process of intellectual borrowing or adaptation in which a person incorporates attractive content or aspects of another culture into the person's own culture.(Spinder,1987). The importance of empowerment of the students and the need for the incorporation of the concepts prompted Aikenhead to propose the term 'autonomous acculturation' in which a student incorporates some contents from western science and technology because the contents appear useful to him/her, thereby replacing some former indigenous views. Everyday thinking is an integrated combination of commonsense thinking and some science education policy in any non-western developing country should be greatly influenced by the technology thinking, according to Aikenhead

(Aikenhead,1997).The process of cultural negotiations could be described as multi science education (Christie,1991, Ogawa 1995).

If ones understanding of science is based on ones worldview then science worldview of the people of that country.

## What Is Worldview

According to Cobern, worldview under girds rationality.(Cobern 2000).To be rational means to think and act with reason or in order words to have an explanation or justification that ultimately rests upon one's pre-suppositions about the world. In order words, a worldview inclines one to a particular way of thinking. The anthropologist,Kearney, asserts that 'the worldview of a people is their way of looking at reality. It consists of basic assumptions and images that provide a more or less coherent, though not necessarily accurate way of thinking about the world' (Kearney,1984). Pre-suppositions are therefore the basic blocks upon which one's worldview develops. These are basically beliefs of a people, generated over years and are sub-consciously retained. Worldviews are culturally-dependent, implicit fundamental organizations of the mind. The implicit organization is composed of predispositions which influence one to feel, think, and act in predictable manners. (Cobern,1991) The study of the culture, values and heritage of a particular people is vital to the appreciation and understanding of their worldview especially in respect of science and technology. According to Kraft (1978) a 'worldview defines the self. It sets the boundaries of who and what I am. It also defines everything that is not me, including my relationships to the human and non-human environments. It shapes one's view of the universe, one's conception of time and space. It influences one's norms and beliefs.' (Kraft, 1978) These are very specific and definitive characteristics of worldviews.

# The Ghanaian Worldview

In his book" Ghana's Heritage of Culture", Kofi Antobam (1963) maintains that no progress can take place without the feet with which most moving objects find stability in the troubled mud of the earth. This is a figurative reference to the existence of hard ground as a prerequisite for progress. It is upon this hard ground that any one wishing to progress must fix his or her feet for a firm take off.

Two important inferences can be deduced:

1. The ground must exist in the lasting values of the peoples' traditions,
2. The feet in question, too must be basic social principles of these traditions, which must of necessity have guided that particular group of people to survive through the ages

In identifying what constitutes the Ghanaian personality, Antobam has noted the following:

a. what has been inherited from the past
b. what is being acquired from the foreign impact on the present
c. what mixture of the above two produces to make it peculiar for preference under the conditions.(Antobam,1963)

The Ghanaian, the I am, or the what I am, referred to by Kraft must have been molded by traditions of culture of culture to up-hold among the many values, beliefs, norms and practices the following:

A. The idea of the existence of one Great God as an integral member of society, as distinct from the western and Christian idea of God staying aloof in heaven in the community of good spirits, looking down on the evil ones in hell, and yet seeking to govern a mixture of the sinners and the righteous on earth;

B. The belief in life after death as a vital source of hope in human existence;

C. The belief in the perpetual existence of life, in which there is a cycle of pregnancy,life, death and a period of waiting in a universal pool of spiritual existence with a subsequent state of re-incarnation, by which it is possible to change one's lot for better or worse;

D. The belief in the sanctity of man as opposed to woman in society;

E. The belief in the idea of man born free from sin and that he remains so until he or she becomes involved in some polluting circumstances in life, as opposed to the Jewish and Christian idea of man born with original sin which he is said to have inherited from his ancestors, Adam and Eve.

F. The ability to produce a child as a necessary factor for the continuance of marriage

G. The importance of marriage as a criterion of social status;

H. The idea of the left hand being symbolically female and obscene to all intents and purposes, and the right hand being male and socially proper;

I. The principle of age as a vital criterion of wisdom;

J. The custom of attributing material property to the person of the female, and the spiritual to those of the male in society;

K. The system of naming the child in which the new born baby takes its first name from that of its spiritual sponsor  at its destiny-offering ceremony at the court of God, its creator ; the second after that of a virtuous person of the father's choice; the third after a word or words descriptive  of the strongest virtue in the nature and character of the virtuous person of the second name which by popular consent and practice of the society is worth emulating by the child.

These and others lend distinction and vitality to establish the 'who I am and the what I am' of the Ghanaian. These also establish the relationships of the Ghanaian to the human and non-human environments; these shape the Ghanaian view of the universe; the conception of time and space; causality; the norms and beliefs and the day to day practices in the community.

The Ghanaian 'who I am and what I am' have been succinctly described by Assimeng (1981) with the following:

a. conformity and blatant eschewing of individual speculations;
b. lack of self-reliance, owing to the pervading
   influence of the extended family system;
c. fetish worship of authority and charismatic leadership;
d. hatred of criticism.

Ghana is still predominantly a rural community. The majority of the inhabitants engage in subsistence farming .Most Ghanaians still remain firmly attached to their traditional cultural values and are very religious.

Among Ghanaians there is a belief that all entities on earth, both living and non-living, posses life, which is composed of two elements—the spirit and matter. Spirits are fleshless and not visible to the ordinary person or the eyes. Because of their high powers they are able to inhabit natural bodies of their choice. Tress, rocks, rivers, water bodies, mountains and others can become their dwelling places. (Kuada, 1999).

The earth itself is considered to be a deity. Hence in state prayers, references are made to her. The earth is female. Eggs, sex organs and all parts of the body involved in the mysterious operation of creation are believed to be endowed with a certain degree of sanctity and accorded some religious awe in the family. Blood and water are also considered sacred. Spilling of blood is thus strictly prohibited. Among the Akans in Ghana, no one can become a chief whose blood has in any way been spilled unnaturally through face marking, accidents or circumcision (Antobam 1963) .

The presence of the earthly gods is explained by the fact that there is a great distance between God, the Creator and man. These earthly gods function as His Deputies and are geographically and functionally decentralized. They are to be served and their guidance south in return for protection, peace, happiness and long life. The One Great God is an integral member of the community

An aspect of the basis for the Ghanaian worldview is the interrelatedness, interconnectedness and interdependence among humans, living and non-living creation. Most other Africans also share this view with the Ghanaians that nothing exists in isolation and that everything is related to every other being or thing. These interrelationship are found in the languages of the people and expressed in various ways such as : 'I am we ;I am because we are—we are because I am, in other words,we are related because I am in you—you are in me' (Goduka, 1999).This view is endorsed by Fitznor (1998) ' Mother Earth and her inhabitants, plants,animals, mineral rocks, insects, and others are all viewed in an interactive way—they are viewed as alive, as having a spirit,as conscious, and as capable of responding to people. They are our relatives. In ceremonies and teaching circles, each of these relatives is discussed in relation to its connection and contribution to healing, wisdom, power and teachings.(Fitznor, 1998).

The identity of the Ghanaian therefore derives from the interdependence of human beings with one another and with the environment, namely nature. The Ghanaian is thus engulfed in social and cultural interactions in the life of t6he community and nature. The spiritual aspect is considered by Richards in the following way:

> 'The traditional African view of the universe is a spiritual whole in which all beings are organically interrelated and independent. The cosmos is sacred and cannot be objectified. Nature is spirit, not to be exploited…All beings exist in reciprocal relationship to one another; we cannot take without giving… the mode of harmony (rather than control) which prevails does not preclude the ability to struggle. Spirit is primary, yet manifests in material being' (Richards, 1980).

This spiritually centered nature is further characterized as 'Firstly there in no espoused doctrine of religion. In indigenous languages the word 'religion' does not exist. To the indigenes religion is an imported intellectual structure; spirituality is however grounded in indigenous communities and in their soil. Instead of the word, religion, the words used refer to a 'way' of living, a tradition of the people, their spiritual wisdoms. This reflects the orientation of spiritual traditions to a process rather than to an intellectual structure.. These are tools for learning and experience, instead of ends in themselves' (Cajete,1994). Indigenous spirituality is differentiated from the other religions. Indigenous spirituality has no historical founder like Christianity, Islam, Buddhism and Confucianism. It is revealed in the sense that it came into existence as a result of human experience of the mystery of the cosmos. In an attempt to solve the mystery of the universe, indigenes everywhere in Africa have asked questions,searched for answers to these questions and come to the conclusion that the mystery must be a supernatural power to whom belongs both the visible and the invisible…It has no written literature, sacred scriptures or creedal forms. It is essentially oral tradition. (Uka, 1991).

These and others together constitute the cornerstone of the Ghanaian worldview generally and in particular on science, which aims at understanding nature

## The Western Worldview

Beliefs of the Judeo-Christian religions have been identified unequivocally by Poole (1998) as the fertile soil within which western science has evolved and flourished since the 17th century. This assertion gives grounds to the observation by the Japanese educator, Watanabe, that 'in the western idea, man was not an ordinary part of nature. He was a special privileged creator and nature was subordinate to him… he was the master of the natural world, which was at his disposal to analyze, examine and make use of… since the natural world and the whole universe were manifestations of God's creation, the study of it was not only a useful but also a highly esteemed endeavor…Such an outlook provided some of the important religious motivation which fostered the development of modern science in the western world. (Watanabe, 1974)

The rise of Christianity had a very big impact in shaping the present western worldview. Thomas Aquinas preached that God had given mankind reason and intellect and the freedom to use them and in the search to understand nature,mankind was thereby glorifying God (Tarnas, 1991). The stand of Aquinas was that 'whatever is known is known in the manner in which we can know it. He established two fundamental principles of all knowledge:

1. Man can know of the world only that which he learns from experiencing the material world;

2. The world is intelligible to rational man. Every thing that exists can be understood. Everything that exists has a set of causes. These causes are known only through man's experience and his reflection upon that experience.

The modern western worldview maintains a rational concrete universe, devoid of spiritual properties and with an empowered mankind using science to extend power and control over the natural world. This worldview has been described variously by many researchers and scholars as characteristically mechanistic, with nature as an object for 'mastery' (Dijksterhuius, 1986; White, 1967; Radhaskrishman, 1967). Words like 'excessively pragmatic, excessively empiricist, excessively scientistic, explorative and elitist' have all been used to characterize western worldview on science. (Cobern, 1991)

In his treatise on *Magic, Science and Curriculum, Bronowoski, (1978)* offers an explanation for the role of science in the interpretation of nature and states 'first, science is not an independent, value-free, dissociated activity which can be carried on apart from the rest of human life, because, second, it is on the contrary, the expression in a very precise form of the species-species human behavior which centers on making plans. Third, there is no distinction between scientific strategies and human strategies in guiding our long-term track on how to live and how to look at the world. Science is a worldview based on the notion that we can plan by understanding. Fourth, science is distinguished from magical views by the fact that refuses to acknowledge the division between two kinds of logic. There is only one logic; it works the same way in all forms of conduct and is not carried out by any kind of formula but by an active view of how you apply the logic of long-term planning strategies to the whole of your life. Finally and most crucially, science is distinguished from earlier forms of trying to achieve a unitary view of the world by the fact that there is only one form of truth in it..

There is no distinction between the logic of magic and other logic sand there is no distinction between means and ends' (Bronowski,1978).

Smolicz and Nunan (1975) look at the scientific worldview as 'the anthropocentric view (man as conqueror and controller of nature through science); the principle of quantification and demystification (science as a rational process for obtaining quantitative information about the world), and the analytical ideal (the assumption that the whole is best understood by a study of its component parts. (Smolicz and Nunan, 1975).

## THE GHANAIAN WORLDVIEW AND WESTERN SCIENCE WORLDVIEW

There are quite a number of cultural values, beliefs, norms, and practices which would accommodate the concept of 'autonomous acculturation' if western science were regarded as: a repository to be raided for what it can contribute to the achievement of practical ends" (Layton, 1993). As Aiken has stated ' the culture of science is understood by pupils, but scientific thinking does not guide their everyday thinking; yet these pupils can do either type of thinking, depending on the context. Thus, a different cultural process can be identified to guide science-teaching strategies, termed 'anthropological instruction of science' (Aikenhead, 1996).This implies that, when pupils learn scientific explanations, they are ably to contextualize those e4xplanations as appropriate to a 'tribe' of scientists and at the same time, these pupils are able to use their pre-conceptions in appropriate everyday contexts, but not in science context. It is important to distinguish those traditional practices, which are based on religious considerations from those which are derived from practices and norms.

There is an old Ghanaian maxim which has it that "a good custom allowed to dominate society for too long is apt to rob life of its vitality, making good men stale".

Certain values and practices could be changed depending on the circumstances and these changes could be due to the impact of foreign practices.

## RELIGIOUS CONSIDERATIONS

A story is told of a father in a Ghanaian farming community who consistently refused to allow his only child, a boy of 12 years to accompany his friends and peers to the forest. On the day he hesitantly allowed his son after persistent pleas to go with his friends, there was an accident in the forest. A big standing tree fell and hit his son on the head, killing him instantly. The grieving father had some questions to answer for himself, among which are:

1. Why did he allow the son to go to the forest with his friends on that particular day although he had consistently refused the request on previous occasions

2. Why did the tree fall, not on anyone among the group but on his only child and son on that particular day of the boy's first joining the group to the forest? He appreciates that when a standing tree falls on to the head of a 12 –year child death may result.

3. Who fell that tree which was standing erect and therefore not dead?.

It is often said that religious considerations dominate the ordering of the daily lives in African societies. It is these religious beliefs of Ghanaians that sustain them and which constitute the fundamental basis of their sense of social identity, values and destiny. (Kuada, 1999).

Cause and effect for the Ghanaian and indeed for Africans, is teleological and not mechanistic as it is for the scientist. Causality is seen in terms of volition and not in terms of mechanistic laws. Things do not ' just happen' in the traditional African society; events have a cause, but that cause is seen in personal terms . (Okebukolosa & Jegede, 1988)

The cause of death is an important issue for consideration since a tragic death through accident is regarded 'unclean'. Gross and persistent violations of the sanctions of the gods and ancestors are often mentioned as grounds for such tragic deaths. Ghanaians believe that babies are a creation of God and that after birth such babies are given to families on loan by God and for special purposes. On the basis of these values parents go to all extent to consult the deities to find out about the character and nature of their babies, the purpose of their creation, their destiny or what the babies will become and even the name to give to them. (Kuamuah, 2002)

For this grieving father the issue is whether a spirit inhabited the tree that fell on his son and if so what was his sin to have made him incur such calamity. The dilemma of the poor bereaved villager cannot be answered from purely scientific, materialistic, reductionistic, exploitive mechanistic, strictly objective, non-personal and dispassionately independent logical ways of the western science worldview. Is it possible for this father to have a strong sense of self, which is needed for empirical investigations, and be detached completely from the non-self? According to Kearney (1984), while the Self- Non-Self relationship with regard to the individual and society may be one of harmony, the individual –nature relationship is one of dominance. This relationship of dominance is considered to have its basis from the Genesis account of creation and is supposed to have influenced the development of experimental science. (Hooykaas, 1972; Glover, 1984).

On the issue of the cause of the falling of the tree without its being physically felled, resorting to mechanistic structure/function would be an easy answer but not so for this Ghanaian who has the belief that trees are not known or expected to fall on their own. The context of the incident must be considered and is mystical for the villager. This man is not present-oriented. His consideration is to find out what he might have done in the past to incur this calamity. He therefore has to consult the gods and his ancestors.

## CONSTRUCTIVISM AND SCIENCE EDUCATION IN GHANA : HUDDLES AND SUPPORTS

Three assertions are upheld under constructivist epistemology:

1. Knowledge is a way of making sense of experience
2. Knowledge is always an interpretation and therefore always fallible and inherently uncertain
3. All interpretations are based on prior knowledge.( Glasersfeld,1989, Good & Schlagel,1992)

Considering the first assertion, sense making is influenced by social and cultural factors in a student's life. (Atwater, 1991, Gallard, 1992, Pomeroy, 1992, Cobern, 1994).Fundamental beliefs about the world exert a powerful influence on how sense is made of events in the world. Understanding could be defined as 'the epistemological or thinking process by which one comes to conceptual comprehension. Knowing is the metaphysical process or processes of apprehension as determined by one's worldview, by which one comes to accept as true or valid that concept one has comprehended. In order words, knowing is believing that such and such is so. (Cobern,1994).

In order to apply the constructivist approach to the science education programmes in Ghana, reference must be made to the fact that meaning is an interpretation based on prior learning which may include various scientific concepts and culturally dependent pre-suppositions or assumptions about what the world is ultimately like and what constitutes first causes. One cannot therefore derive any meaning without due cognition of the worldview of the learner, since worldview has a great influence on learning. Teachers should not overlook or put aside the beliefs of their students. It is this ignorance of the main tenets of cultural constructivism that accounts for the seemingly ineffective science teaching in Ghana. Cobern opines that though belief is itself an improper goal, it is the place where instruction should begin (Cobern, 1994). He argues that the use of metaphysical questions can be used for discussion in class to raise the students' interests. These questions can be raised for discussion among the students themselves and with the teachers, the outcome of which would be a shared understanding or meaning in the classroom.

The question of belief in teaching and learning must not be under simplified. Belief and understanding are distinct concepts, each of which is a potential goal for instruction. Teachers should therefore accept that while understanding is critical, belief is not, and that belief is up to the students. Beliefs may change and may develop. However the issue of belief cannot be sidestepped if conceptual understanding is to be achieved. One cannot gain much understanding in something one does not believe in. What counts as believable for an individual would depend on that individual's worldview. Since teaching and learning has to take note of the context, metaphysics and worldview cannot be left out.

Science and science teaching are encumbered by many non-scientific ideas. (Thelan, 1983, Fourez, 1988, Linder, 1992).Ghanaian students do have many of such non-scientific ideas derived from their worldview. The legitimate and positive role of belief in the science classroom should be recognized and be encouraged. Teachers could therefore preface conceptual study of science with a classroom dialogue relating to material on beliefs and cultural history and factors of those topics, if available. Cultural constructivist approach therefore seems relevant in the Ghanaian situation.

Constructivism is itself a construct of western science education research (Gough,1998) and its incorporation into the learning practices of the Ghanaian student would need efficient management, provision of trained science teachers in the constructivist theory and availability of relevant teaching and learning materials in order to create an atmosphere for change.

Placing science in context is fundamental to the constructivist idea of learning. The theory directs the teacher to recognize that every student will build upon an existing knowledge framework and accept or reject new ideas in the context of what he or she knows. No knowledge can occur if there is no foundation on which to pin it. In order words, to remember something means having some sort of 'memory hook'. (Stocklmayer, 2001) The emphasis is on constructing one's knowledge based on previous knowledge. This also reflects on the need for relevance. According to Driver v(1986), learning outcomes depend not only on the learning environment but also on the knowledge of the learner . Construction of a meaning is influenced to a large extent by one's existing knowledge. The learning environment involves participation and collaboration. This is where the Ghanaian student falls short. Cooperation and collaboration with others are not among the known characteristic of the Ghanaian. Doing it alone is his method.

Yager (1991 ) considers the ' pinning' as building on and states "explaining a problem will not lead to understanding unless the learning has an internal scheme that maps onto what a person is hearing. Learning is the product of self-organization and re-organization" The idea of pinning on demands that students are given the opportunities to make sense of what is learned by negotiating meaning ; comparing what is known to new experiences, and resolving discrepancies between what is known and what seems to be implied by new experiences. (Tobin, 1990)

Science educators are exhorted by Cobern to use a constructivist model of learning to both support the need for and to facilitate investigations of how science education can be formulated from different cultural perspectives. (Cobern, 1996)

With respect to the Ghanaian, the grounds to pin on are the Ghanaian worldview, while the new experiences would mostly be the western science. If participation learning or collaborative learning is the real essence of constructivism, then it would be very difficult for the Ghanaian student to benefit fr5om this theory in view of his inherent attitude to the learning process. He is generally acquiescent, eschews individual speculation and lacks self-reliance and in addition engages in worshipping authority and age. (Assimeng, 1981). He expects knowledge to be passed down from the teacher who is supposed to be knowledgeable and who by virtue of age is the custodian of wisdom and must be respected. Or the Ghanaian student to be able to change his non-participatory attitude to the learning process, he would need an effective teacher to facilitate the border crossing between his own worldview and the new experiences from the western science. To achieve effective participatory learning, Yager (1991) recommends the following among others:

a. Using open-ended questions
b. Encouraging participants to suggest causes for
   particular events and predictions of consequences
c. Encouraging the testing of the participants own
   ideas including answering their own guesses.
d. Encouraging participants to challenge conceptions and ideas.
e. Using cooperative strategies that emphasize collaboration,
   respect for the individual and use of labor division.

f.  Encouraging self-analysis, collection of real evidence to support ideas and reformation in the light of new experiences.

Other situations,which would make the participatory learning process difficult to practice in the Ghanaian classroom, include

i.  Large class sizes,
ii.  Insufficient textbooks and reading materials,
iii. Presence of untrained teachers who lack confidence in themselves,
iv. Poor supervision.

The cultural practice relating the social status of the male over that of the female would also have to be recognized as it would create an obstacle for effective participatory learning in a n co-educational institution.

Even where the sexes are separated  the other factors need to be addressed. In order to encourage more female students to study science and mathematics the Ghana Education Service  instituted the Science, Technology and Mathematics Education (STME) clinics  for girls. Through these clinics more girls were encouraged to study science  and thus increasing the class sizes without the corresponding increase  in logistical support. This approach  emphasized the 'scientistic' view and disregarded the traditional culture relating to the status of the female in the society. In such a situation, traditional culture, which discourages females doing science was considered the culprit for the lack of technological development. Anamuah-Mensah seems to uphold this view. He contends 'it is my view that previous initiatives to harness science and technology for development have not been successful; they have not made development a reality, instead development has become a mirage due to the neglect of what I consider to be the most important development source, the feminine citizenry. I believe that the inclusion of females in the development equation will make development a reality instead of a mirage' (Anamuah-Mensah, 2000). Anamuah-Mensah bases his thinking on the fact that since in the traditional society women contribute significantly to the production of food, food processing, and marketing, their study of science and technology would help in the development programme. This view is shortsighted and naïve. The contribution of science and technology for development that is being advocated is based on the western science, a very different worldview from the traditional Ghanaian worldview, which has a whole set of roles for the Ghanaian woman.

Even in the western industrialized countries it is recognized that more males take to science than females. Various reasons have been advanced for that situation (Head,1985). Mahatma Gandhi said of a woman trying to behave as a man thus' she can run the race but she will not rise to the heights she is capable of by mimicking men.' (Gandhi, 1940) In the Ghanaian situation there are many factors to be considered when it comes to the issue of development. It is very unrealistic to put the blame on the paucity of females with knowledge of the western science and technology. To be preaching ' science first' without any consideration of the cultural milieu will not be fruitful. It must be realized that science has a cultural dimension and that the issue is more cultural than sociological. From the feminist literature, it is argued, " the problem is not making women more scientific, but making science less masculine", (Fee, 1981)

In the classroom teachers may unconsciously accept science's gender-role stereotypes and reinforce this by their attitudes. As such the cultural practice whereby, right from infancy boys and girls are treated differently and which instills in the boys a dominant role .According to Rich (1979), 'If there is any misleading concept, it is that of co-education;(to consider that) because women and men are sitting in the same classroom hearing the same lecture, reading the same books, performing the same laboratories, they are receiving the same education. They are not'. Unless teachers are made constantly aware of such issues especially in a male dominated society, like Ghana, the boys and girls may experience a subtle gender-laden education and the already masculine image that science portrays may be intensified. The masculine image of science cannot be altered without the re-conceptualization of what is masculine and feminine. (Keller, 1987) .The attitude of students to learning science is greatly impacted by their gender constructions about self and subject. In the Ghanaian community the boys and girls are very much aware of their different cultural roles .They enter the classroom with different knowledge, self-confidence and expectations about their ability to learn. Special strategies may have to be evolved to change the image of science as a male's domain in order to assist the female students to alter their views of science and their ability to participate.

The constructivist theory can be utilized to make learning meaningful in some situations in the Ghanaian environment.( Brown-Acquaye,2001)

These include:

## Concept Of Pro-creation/Reproduction

The traditional Ghanaian believes that it is the mother who is responsible for the blood *(mbogya)*, which is to be the <u>material</u> part of the child. The father gives the <u>spirit and personality</u> *(sunsum)*.It is through sexual intercourse that the *sunsum* is transmitted. The final exercise of procreation is completed when God, the Creator brings life to the child by quickening it with its soul *(okera)*, which is <u>the sustainer and the conscience of life</u>. The soul is handed to the child as the last ceremony and aspect of its creation and these occur just instantaneously before its birth. The child becomes a human being only at birth and not during pregnancy (Antobam, 1963).Babies are a creation of God and are given to families on loan and for special purposes. Hence it is only God who can take away life. The first seven days after birth are considered a transition period between pre-birth and the world of living. It is on the eight day that the baby crosses the boundary into the world of living. This pro-creation belief underscores the religious nature of the Ghanaian and does not call for the explanation of the mystery involved. In the western worldview, no mention is made of the presence of the soul in the human body in explaining reproduction, although the Judeo-Christian religion, upon which the western worldview depends, acknowledges the existence of the soul in the human body. The topic on the creation hinges on beliefs and as such the metaphysical questions can be used as part of the introductory discussion to arrive at a shared meaning The acceptance of the notion of blood in the baby as the material part of pro-creation exercise should afford the opportunity to ' raid the repository' for what it can contribute to the physical and chemical composition of blood, an exercise which is the domain of western science. This approach would open up a whole series of topics in western science relating to

1. blood,its composition, its functions in the body, its relevance
2. the structure of the body itself, its

    anatomy, physiology and others

To achieve a successful negotiation and facilitate easy border crossing, it should be made abundantly clear to the students that their own worldview does not offer any explanation nor elaborate on the composition of that material part, the blood and that another worldview, namely that of western science is being introduced to elucidate the structure,physical and chemical composition of the blood in the baby. Under such a situation the existing knowledge of the Ghanaian students in relation to pro-creation is being used to build on new knowledge which does not in any way challenge or marginalize their previous knowledge.

The belief and practice whereby during the first seven days, the child should be kept indoors and outsiders prevented from seeing and handling it could also be used to explain the frailty of the newborn baby and the consequences and hazards of exposure of the baby to diseases.

Here again a whole spectrum of topics and concepts drawn from western science can be raised and discussed. These topics could cover:

i. causes and prevention of diseases
ii. germs
iii. hygiene
iv. cleanliness and sanitation
v. nutrition.

Here too the approach is to build on their previous knowledge and experiences which are not being marginalized or replaced by the new western ideas. The link between the transition period and infant mortality can easily be established

Menstruation is another topic which can be linked to the procreation exercise. Among the Akans and other tribes, the first menstrual period of the girls calls for celebration. This first occurrence is considered as a sign that the girl is of age. This stage of maturity among of the girls is marked by special marriage or nobility rite According to the Ghanaian practice, men are expected to avoid women with menstrual blood or ceremonies associated with it. This is based on their understanding that women in their menstrual period are a source of danger to people who have certain powers and include chiefs, traditional priests, diviners and *jujumen* .It is believed that the menstrual blood neutralizes the powers of these people. Building on this special attitude to menstruation, one can utilize western science to

a. explain the menstrual cycle of females
b. significance of menstruation and its role in the reproduction process.

## Rivers, Water- Bodies, Rocks, Mountains, Planetary System

All entities on earth, both living and non-living are believed to possess life. Life is composed of two elements- the spirit and matter. Spirits are normally fleshless and therefore not visible to the ordinary person or eyes. Because of their high powers they are able to inhabit natural objects of their choice. Trees, rocks, river-bodies, mountains etc. can therefore become their dwelling places. These spirits and gods are venerated and worshiped. The veneration is not for the dwelling places. These places are however protected with sanctions and taboos to ensure their stability as dwelling places for the gods (Kuada, 1999). Of the two elements that constitute life no explanation is given in the Ghanaian beliefs about the physical and chemical composition of matter. It is quite conceivable to employ western science to explain the composition of these natural objects and places, which the gods inhabit. The following topics can be discussed:

- The location and paths of rivers, their importance to the community for the provision of water and fish,
- The chemical composition of water, its purification,
- Pollution of the river and water bodies
- Fish – its physiology, anatomy and importance as source of protein
- What protein is and the natural needs of mankind.

The presence of these gods in the localities is to ensure the protection and survival of the communities. There are prescribed ceremonies, which involve sacrifices for permission to invade on the 'privacy' of the gods. The Volta River has been dammed to create the Volta Lake for hydroelectricity generation using western technology, and this was done after the prescribed sacrifices and ceremonies had been done.

The composition of rocks, both physical and chemical, the formation of rocks through chemical combination of elements, reaction of elements and compounds etc. can all be taught with western science. The utilization of these natural resources can be highlighted for the provision of houses, furniture through western technology.

In respect of trees, a whole series to topics can be listed including:

- Botany
- Ecology
- Forestry
- Biodiversity
- Herbal plants
- Zoology

Certain herbs are known by the herbalists to make body bullet-proof, injury-free and pain-free. These herbalists have knowledge of the herbs and a study of their composition and properties with western science could be encouraged.

The local Ghanaian fishermen have extensive and comprehensive knowledge for the stars and the planetary systems which they use daily in the vocation. This traditional knowledge of the stars and the planetary system is passed on to the children, the majority of whom later take to fishing as vocation. To subject these children to learn "The

Night Sky over Ghana" from western astronomy without any basis for that study, alienates the pupils. What would be more meaningful and beneficial to the pupils is to introduce them to the use of binoculars, the groupings of the stars and the planetary systems made by the local fishermen would be better observed. Improved observation of the stars would rather endear the pupils to learn the western science. Topics that could easily be introduced without alienating the students include:

- Light and optics
- The eyes and lenses
- Refraction and reflection
- The color of the sky and rainbow

## USE OF THE LEFT AND RIGHT HANDS

In the Ghanaian culture, the left hand is used for filthy things, for example cleaning of oneself after visiting the toilet, collecting dirty items or rubbish etc. Symbolically the left hand is regarded as female and has to do with maternal part of life, while the spiritual part is male and thus assigned to the right hand. Hence it is an insult to attempt to shake hands with the left hand to drop one's left hand into food and to present or receive gifts with the left hand. This attitude and practice have serious implications for the Ghanaian science student who needs both hands equally in experimental science.

The fact that the Ghanaian ancestors assigned specific functions to the different hands is an indication of their awareness of diseases and their causes and how to avoid infection. After explaining the cultural aspects of the use of the hands, western science could be invoked to explain;

- The anatomy of the hands, their similarities and functions
- Chemistry of soaps and detergents
- Germs and infection
- Sanitation

The preparation of local soaps from local raw materials such as palm oil, coconut oil and the solution from the ashed plantain peels could be discussed and compared with the preparation of soaps from western science. It could be pointed out that soaps prepared from western science have higher potency to kill germs and thus thoroughly cleansing of both hands with soaps would prevent spread of diseases equally on each hands.

## Values And Attitudes With Respect To Age And Authority

Africans in general and Ghanaians in particular have the tendency to equate age with the possession of wisdom. "The general view is that the elderly have proved their strength in the face of all the destructive forces of life and have lived in harmony with the ancestral spirits and nature. Their wealth of experience carries with it natural authority and respect" (Kuade, 1999). Because of this belief, children are not expected to participate in conversation with their elders unless directly addressed. They are to listen and learn from the elders. This attitude is carried over into adult life and practiced. Students in class will not participate in class discussions voluntarily. Teachers are held in high esteem since they are considered to be highly to as 'Sir, Miss or Madam'. This attitude falls in line with the characteristic behaviour of the Ghanaian being unquestioningly acquiescent and prepared to take whatever instruction or directives given by the elders, teachers and authority. This has serious implications for school administration where members of staff, both academic and administrative will stand aloof and look up to the Headmaster, Principal or the Vice-Chancellor for instructions and directives. Post graduate students studying either locally or at overseas universities are also affected by this non-questioning attitude. They are very unwilling to engage in nay serious academic discussion with their professors and supervisors. By this nature Ghanaians prefer the status quo and would not wish to alter any unfavourable situation, if by so doing he might jeopardize his continuous stay at the university.

It is therefore not surprising to find some of these students returning home after their studies to humbly carry on and propagate the ideas and vision of their overseas professors regardless of the cultural implications. Some of these may even invite their overseas professors or supervisors to come down to Ghana to run workshops in such areas as 'mentoring' to student teachers; 'computer assisted learning' to academic staff when it is clear that the infrastructure and logistical support for computer assisted learning are not available. Mentoring cannot be divorced from the cultural settings and these invited professors may be very ignorant of the culture of their audiences.

Another problem, which could be related to the cultural disorientation, arises from the fact that students apply for and gain admission for post-graduate studies overseas to study under professors who may nothing of the cultural background of their prospective students apart from the academic qualifications. These students also have no idea of the cultural settings they would be exposed in the overseas universities. In order to satisfy his professor, this newly arrived; highly motivated student adopts one of the strategies identified by Cohen and Blanc (1996). In view of his ignorance of the ways and manners about how things are done in his new environment, this student would comfortably resort to 'doing school', and try as much as possible to conform to the university culture under severe stress.

His appreciation of the role of his professor in his educational advancement may lead him to name one of his children after the professor or supervisor. A more pervasive influence on the Ghanaian student would be his effort to interpret his research findings and data to conform to the wishes and desires of his professor or supervisor and tot their stereotypical image of events. For example, Europeans and Americans have a stereotypical image of the high incidence of teenage pregnancy in Africa. It is therefore easy to attribute high drop out rate of Ghanaian girls from primary to junior secondary school and from secondary school to senior secondary school to partly teenage pregnancy and low performance. No explanation is given to the similarly high dropout rate for boys. In Zanzibar, an island off the eastern coast of Africa in the Indian Ocean, it was found that the attrition rates in science at the secondary school level were lower for girls than boys. Only 1000 girls dropped out for marriage and only 1 in 10,000 for pregnancy (Naidoo, 1998). What could be the reasons for these high disparities in the drop out rates for these African students in these two different countries, one of which, Zanzibar is strongly Moslem country. Head (1985) states 'people are likely to pay attention and get involved in activities which they expect to be interesting, rewarding or worthwhile in some way'. What is interesting for the Ghanaian girls to stay at school? In the Ghanaian tradition great premium is placed on the ability to produce a child, a necessary factor for the continuation of marriage, which is a criterion of social status in the Ghanaian community. This is why most ethnic groups in  Ghana perform girls' nobility rites to signify the point at which a girl is considered mature for marriage. That point is the time when the girl begins to menstruate. It is not just a customary performance but also a great celebration. Among the Akans in Ghana, where the survival of the matrilineage depends on its female members, a barren woman is in disgrace and despair. Prolific child bearing is honored and parents of large families and mothers of twins and triplets are held in special esteem (Sarpong, 1977). According to Fortes, 'the idea of an unwanted pregnancy in marriage is unheard of. An Ashanti countrywoman would be horrified at the suggestion of an induced miscarriage. This applies to even unmarried girl'. The idea of every Ashanti or for that matter Akans to have as many children as life permits. It could be deduced that the drop out rate for girls has more to do with cultural values than its being placed within the stereotype negative image.

Science and technology are powerful cultural forces, but their ability to cause changes in those attitudes and behaviours that are based on religious beliefs may be minimal and may take a long time to cause the desired changes in  beliefs. It should not be forgotten that science and technology are relatively new imports into the culture of all the developing countries and thus the school education 'separates science from pupils' everyday lives, and in particular their non-school knowledge of the natural world. It is learnt primarily as a laboratory activity, in a room full of special rules, many of which have no real necessity except in terms of the social organization of the school (Young, 1976). Special efforts need to be taken if these attitudes are to be changed so that the learning processes could benefit from the constructivist approach. It is possible to effect these changes but it needs planning by the teachers.

## The Language Factor

A major problem with the teaching of science is with its communicating. The possibility of communicating the wrong idea is very high and this would leave the students more puzzled than before. The Ghanaian students already consider science to be 'hard' and difficult to understand and also not very important for real life. Learning of science is considered to be done by rote acquisition of facts and formulae, which have no bearing or relevance to their daily lives. Learning science is made more difficult if it has to be taught in English, a second language, by teachers whose knowledge of the English language as shallow.

In all learning processes, the medium of instruction has a major role to play since it is related to both attitude and cognition. In Ghana knowledge of the English language commands a prestigious position as it provides access to jobs and economic power. The image of science is complicated by the need to gain control over the English language.

A lot of studies have been done on the challenges of learning science through a second language like English. Two categories of learners of science using English as the medium has been identified (Strevens, 1980),

i. Those who have come to an English-speaking country having received part or all of their knowledge in another language and
ii. Those who are citizens of a multi-lingual country where the language of official communication is English and who are officially taught at school through the medium of English.

The Ghanaian falls into the second category and encounters English for the first time at school. Text books are written in English, class assignments are to be done in English and examinations are also conducted in English. Krashen (1982) distinguishes between language, learning and language acquisition and associates those in the second category above, like the Ghanaians to be more engaged with language learning. Because of the slow and ineffective start with the second language, there is bound to be a mixture of language acquisition and language learning for its category.

There is a contrast between conversational academic language proficiency for the second category, Cummins (1980). This group has difficulty in expressing ideas in writing. They can articulate an oral understanding of a concept but have difficulties in communicating these ideas on paper. The members in this group are therefore found to give the general ideas on paper. The members in this group are therefore found to give the general impression of poor performance at written examinations. From his studies (Rutherford 1993) considers problems associated with expressing scientific ideas in African languages have more to do with vocabulary, logical connectors and multiple meanings of words. Conceptual difficulties in learning science have also been identified. The qualities of the writing skills of students are related to their conceptual understanding of the content of the science assignment. The inference is that poorly written science assignments may be due wither to poor language proficiency or weak conceptual understanding (Inglis, 1993). Similar observation has been made which includes traditional thinking and culture as also impacting on science language (Rollnick et al 1992). They state that 'the student in Africa has one name which is used at school and another name which is used at home. There is one type of acceptable behaviour at school and one at home. There is one type of dress for school and one for home. There is a language for school and language for home. Because of this the student too becomes two people. Language us indeed part of the learner's culture and words and meanings are based on cultural backgrounds.

Oral transmission as a means of passing knowledge from general to generation also has effects on learning science. Certain conventions are important in the oral transmission as they mediate thought processes and may not be compatible with or acceptable in scientific writings. Although literacy is on the increase among Ghanaians the rate in too slow to overshadow oral transmission. From their studies in Botswana, have observed that scientific concepts attainments are greatly influenced by the language of instruction (Prophet and Dow, 1994). Collison has also noted that the Ghanaian pupils made higher cognitive level statements in class discussions when they used the local home language than when they used English language, the official language of instruction (Collison).

From a theoretical consideration of the role of the language instruction in science teaching and learning, it is evident that in a situation where that language is a second language for students, there would be considerable difficulties in the teaching and learning processes.

It is therefore unfortunate that the concept of science for development is still accepted by the government even up to today.

## THE TEACHER AS A CULTURAL BROKER

The role of the teacher as a cultural broker in the autonomous acculturation model is very vital. The teachers would have to know and decide when to cross the borders and how to raid the repertoire of western science.

For a successful border crossing the teachers must be very knowledgeable in the local culture and traditions, values and norms that underpin the students' world view. Jegede refers to a 'conceptual eco-cultural' paradigm as "a state in which the growth and development of an individual's perception of knowledge is drawn from the socio-cultural environment in which the learner lives and operates (Jegede, 1995). The eco-cultural paradigm is to acknowledge cultural differences, provide emotional support for pupils and to set the stage for cross-cultural instruction. In this way the pupils would feel empowered and feel at ease.

The extent of the skills of the teachers as cultural brokers is an index of the success of the autonomous acculturation process. The teacher's role is to guide the students move between their life-world culture and the culture of science and assist them to settle any conflicts. His role is as that of a coordinator, facilitator and resource person in multicultural education (Atwater, 1996). Teachers must be made aware that even in situations where the crossing is made easy, certain factors such as lack of motivation, interest, teaching and learning materials, might create other problems that would be at odds with school science. The teachers must always attempt to answer the question: How do we modify this western concept to fit into the students' pre-existing knowledge? Teachers must avoid distorting the local knowledge by making it conform to the western school science. The approach is to bring western science into students' worldview rather than making the students construct the world view of the western scientist. The goal of the teacher as a cultural broker must be to ensure that the students feel comfortable in both cultures and that they are able to commute between the two cultures without headaches. Fleer (1997) maintains that 'moving between world views creates high level thinkers'. Under the present situation in Ghana the teaching of western science is the practice and has no regard to the culture of the students. Wholesale transfer of scientific facts and data is emphasized for the purpose of passing examinations. The introduction of the autonomous acculturation model into the science education program would be a way to change direction in the educational policy. After the teachers have achieved some success in their roles as cultural brokers they could be introduced to that new perspective proposed by Taylor and Cobern (1998), which is described as 'critical enculturation'. Culture is dynamic and hence 'critical enculturation' would not be too much off the mark since it would involve "a dialectical view of the process of cultural adaptation and which must recognize the need for reciprocal accommodation of the beliefs, values and practices of modern science and the host culture. (Taylor and Cobern, 1998).

## CONCLUSION

The way that science is being taught in Ghana is not enabling the students to appreciate science and to have meaningful learning. Neither is science and technology having impact on the nation for industrialization and development due to the way science and technology are taught. Ghana cannot continue to be just a consumer nation, one that imports finished products and exports raw materials. New ways of teaching must be evolved. Ways that recognize the cultural aspects of science, the culture and traditions of the teachers and the students alike are the most viable means to ensure meaningful teaching and learning. Autonomous acculturation seems to be a viable method, which can be employed without many difficulties. This process has good potential for making science education realistic and relevant in Ghana. The need for educators to recognize and appreciate the cultural milieu in which the students' beliefs, values and relationships are grounded and supported is paramount for effective teaching and learning using the constructivist approach. By this means any resistance to science learning can be interpreted and contained. One could ascertain whether it is the science per se which is being resisted or it is the context of the science being taught which is the obstacle. Answers to these questions would be useful in the sense that the success of science education depends on the extent "that science can find a niche in the cognitive and socio-cultural milieu of the students" (Cobern, 1994).

Teaching is cultural transmission while learning is cultural acquisition (Contrereras and Lee, 1990), and hence one would need a sort of 'contextually modified' constructive theory to make learning meaningful for the Ghanaian student.

Jenkins (1992) has commented that using science in everyday worlds "is about creating new knowledge, or where possible, restructuring, re-working and transforming existing scientific knowledge into forms which serve the purpose in hand. Whatever that purpose (political, social, personal etc.), it is essentially concerned with action or capability, rather than with acquisition of knowledge for its own sake" (Jenkins, 1992).

The Ghanaian believes in one supreme God, the Creator of the universe just like the western Christian. The differences between the two cultures are more on attitudes to this creator than on theological grounds. While the western Christian is exploiting the material resources on nature for development the Ghanaian may be said to be indifferent to material development and to be interested in spiritual and religious development. It is the balance between these two aspects of attitudes to the Creator. While the physical and material developments are visible and impressive, the spiritual and religious may not be discernable to the ordinary person. Some aspects of both are however needed. If great water-bodies like the Great Lakes in America, if such big rivers like the Mississippi, Hudson, Thames, Reine, which in the Ghanaian mythology all could be dwelling places of other entities created by the same Almighty God, if great mountains like The Alps, could be excavated, if trees would be cleared, all for the purpose of making life on earth more comfortable and the 'godly' inhabitants of these places have looked kindly to their exploration, one may wonder why a change in the Ghanaian attitude to nature cannot be made. There are a lot of mining activities in Ghana, which involve both surface and underground activities and no overt sanctions from the spirits and gods who inhabit those places have been experiences. The timber industry in Ghana, regardless of the negative environmental degradation involve due to the felling of the trees, has not attracted any sanctions from the deities who dwell there. It is known that before any of these big industrial ventures are undertaken, special prayers and sacrifices are made to the gods and the spirits. These should be highlighted as a way to prove to the Ghanaians that the spirits and the gods in the community are there on a mission from the Almighty whom they represent to protect and guide the people and community.

Just as for the physical and material development of Ghana through the use of science and technology has found the constructivist theory based on western worldview relevant, useful and appropriate at this time in time, it is hoped that the relatively low consideration given to the spiritual and religious domains in nature by the western world be uplifted by learning from those underdeveloped countries where spiritual considerations seems to be paramount in their world views.

Universities in Ghana should be made to identify overseas professors who have some ideas about the Ghanaian worldview and culture. It is these professors who should be recommended to supervise prospective post-graduate students from Ghana. Similarly students granted scholarships for overseas studies should be well briefed about their supervisors and professors. This strategy can be useful if pains are taken by the universities in Ghana to cooperate within themselves and establish links with overseas universities collectively.

Since constructivism as a theory is very relevant for science teaching it is important that science teachers have good understanding of the theory. The cultural relevance in teaching through constructivist approach must also be thoroughly understood by the science teachers. Unfortunately most of the science education lecturers in Ghana do not employ the constructivist theory in teaching. Ziman (1991) admonishes that 'appropriate scientific knowledge is not received impersonally, as the product of disembodied expertise, but comes as part of life, among real people with real interest in a real world (Ziman, 1991).

In the present situation in the developing countries where poverty, diseases and ignorance stare in the faces of the citizens, it is only through hard work, dedication and perseverance that the hopes and aspirations of the people can be raised. As Ghana's sages have said, "it gives the teeth of a child more strength to struggle for naught with the hard bone of a chicken's foot than to fiddle for sweetness with a piece of soft sugar cane".

# CHAPTER TWO:
# SCIENCE FOR DEVELOPMENT IN AFRICA

## THE CASE OF FAILURE IN GHANA

### Introduction

In all the developing countries of the Third World, particular Africa, signs of extreme poverty, poor sanitation, lack of safe potable water, diseases, poor housing, poor health services, high infant mortalities and low life expectancy are very visible.

Many governments of the industrialized countries, international NGOs and agencies of the United Nations have expressed concerns for these deplorable situations, which are mostly preventable. Unfortunately the governments of these developing countries are incapable of solving or alleviating the problems. Therefore offer of any assistance from any quarter is most welcome to them. Rarely do they the recipient governments question the motives for the offers, the appropriateness of the interventions and the implications for accepting the offers.

The visible signs of economic and social developments in the western industrialized countries are very attractive and appealing to the developing countries. Of late, quite high on the agenda for fast track development in the developing countries is the notion that only scientific knowledge and exogenous technologies can provide the panacea for their problems. Hitchhiking on the fast lane of the current information technology through the internet is most desirable.

We are referring to citizens of the developing countries, the majority of whom are illiterates in science and technology without any access to good potable water or to electricity or to good housing but whose government officials have been trained in the western industrialized countries and have exogenous inclinations and believe in and accept the concept of science for development, one of the many intervention programmes introduced to stem the deterioration of the prevailing conditions. The UN and its specialized agencies, like UNESCO, FAO, UNDP and other international donor agencies, have championed this concept of 'science for development'.

## SCIENCE FOR DEVELOPMENT MODEL IN GHANA

Long before the adoption of the concept of 'science for development', first President of the Republic of Ghana, Dr. Kwame Nkrumah had some genuine belief in the potency of science and technology to propel Ghana, and for that matter the whole of Africa, into modern, civilized, industrialized and economically vibrant society. He must have been influenced greatly during his study periods in the USA and Britain.

Immediately after independence in 1957, he initiated many programmes based on science and technology for the rapid industrialization of Ghana. The University of Science and technology, now named after him (Kwame Nkrumah University of Science and Technology), was established in 1961. This was followed in 1962 with the establishment of the University College of Science Education, now called the University of Cape Coast, which was mandated to produce only graduate teachers in science for the secondary schools in Ghana. Next follow was the Ghana Atomic Commission, established at Kwabenya near the premier university, University of Ghana. To support these academic and research institutions, The Ghana Industrial Holding Corporation (GIHOC), comprising of sixteen (16) different industries was established about the same period.

Unfortunately when the government of Dr. Kwame Nkrumah was over thrown through a military coup d'etat in 1966, all the developmental programmes initiated were jettisoned overboard and since then no coordinated programmes based on science and technology have been presented.

One would question whether the programmes initiated by Dr. Nkrumah based on science and technology would have been successful had his government not been overthrown. The answer could be Yes or No.

Consideration that Nkrumah's government became dictatorial, operating in a one-party state with himself as the life president, the chances of pushing through all the programmes to success are imaginable. He had succeeded to build Akosombo dam to create Volta Lake, which up to date is the largest man made lake in the world to generate cheap hydroelectric power to be used in the production of aluminum from bauxite.

Although Drori (Cobern 1998, p.56) successfully debunks the notion of a casual link between science and technology for economic progress from case studies of the newly industrialized countries (NIC), the case of Malaysia was exception. Malaysia and Ghana both gained their respective independence status from Britain in the same year, 1957, with Ghana three months earlier. Just as Ghana under Kwame Nkrumah, had a strong centrally controlled economy in a dictatorial regime Malaysia had a similar environment. In Malaysia, Lewis (1993) reports "access to science education is near universal at primary level and the quality of teaching and material resources in becoming comparable to that found in industrialized countries." Under Nkrumah's government similar conditions prevailed. Incentives were given to students to study science in the universities. The allowances for students studying were higher than those given to non-science students. Science that time enjoyed such high legitimacy and status that Dr. Kwame Nkrumah, the President instituted the Ghana Academy of Science, which has now been extended to cover the Arts and known as the Ghana Academy of Arts and Sciences.

Now, Malaysia is one of the newly industrialized countries, which has transformed itself since 1971 from a producer of raw material into an emerging multi-sector economy with electronics as one of its main export products to the USA and Japan. As at the year 2000 internet users in Malaysia numbered 4.1 million (CIA Doc.). With a healthy foreign exchange reserves and relatively small external debt, Malaysia is presently way ahead of Ghana which could only boast of only 200,000 internet users as at the year 2000. Ghana remains heavily dependent on international finance and technical assistance and with its present economic harassment had no choice but to opt for debt relief under the Heavily Indebted Poor Country (HIPC) programme in 2000.

The differences in the situations in the two countries can only be explained by the political instability in the case of Ghana and the presence of a strong stable government in Malaysia. Also to be noted is the fact that whereas both Ghana and Malaysia had Britain colonial masters, Ghana retained and still uses English, a foreign language, as the official language and the language of instruction in schools. Malaysia uses a local language, Bahasa Melayu as the official language and that for instruction in schools.

Dr. Kwame Nkrumah strongly believed in Pan-Africanism and worked very hard towards the unification of Africa under a Union government. In his drive for the African Unity he had problems with some leaders of the other newly independent African countries on policy issues and ideological grounds. Nkrumah had socialist inclinations while some of the other Head of States, particularly Nigeria at that time has capitalist tendencies. The colonial masters, particularly France, did not leave their newly independent states free to do what they wanted. They had an agenda for them and advocated for 'assimilation' with France. The British however acted differently leaving their former colonies to their own fates, designs and aspirations. Nevertheless, Nkrumah was very skeptical of these former colonial masters and feared that they had schemes to perpetually bind them economically as neo-colonialist states.

A study of the conceptual model of science for development for use in the developing countries would lead one to concur with the skepticism of Kwame Nkrumah. The adoption of the science for development model in Ghana and elsewhere was to frustrate the drive towards the development of a truly industrialized Ghana, directing its own research and development programmes. Nkrumah's dreams would have been stillborn.

## CONTEXTUAL HURDLES IN THE GHANAIAN SITUATION

Regardless of whatever might have happened under Kwame Nkrumah's government, a very detailed analyses of the implementation of the conceptual model of science and technology for development have been provided by Dori (Cobern, 1998), which, citing from empirical studies clearly 'contradict our everyday notion of science education and the predictions made by the model of science education for development'. From their own studies Kamens and Benavot (1991, p.166) report that "it does not appear that official attention given to mathematics and science instruction in primary education is directly related to key indications of socio-economic development, economic dependence or world system position. The casual link between science and education and economic development is at best mythical".

Cultural barriers are mentioned among some social mechanisms that impede the success of the science for development model and Drodi points out that 'such barriers impede the transfer of knowledge-knowledge that was created in a particular cultural context and thus is value – and symbol-laden-to another cultural sphere". (Drori, Cobern, 1998 p.62)

Many cultural barriers do exist in the Ghanaian situation to stifle the implementation of the science for development concept. According to Benavot (1999, p.173) 'the economic effect of science education may have more to do with "hidden" cultural rules, orientations and worldviews being transmitted than with the specific content being taught.' The current push towards globalization necessities would view standardization of scientific education curricula and isomorphism (Drori, p.59). The role of science education, according to Drori, is two fold within the scheme of science education for development:

a) To shape positive attitudes modernization and
b) To train candidates in science and technology and prepare them for higher education and for sophisticated production roles" (Drori, p.35). within the science for development model there is provision for professional training and for the provision of local skilled labour for the economy.

Unfortunately this conceptual frame of science for developments based on western science whose view, according to Cobern is grounded on the following three imperatives of modern society:

i. the imperative of Naturalism – all phenomenon can ultimately and adequately be understood in naturalistic terms.

ii. The scientific imperative – anything than can be studied, should be made. (Cobern, p.20)

From the above statements it is evident that the single logical goal of the western world view is the material well being of the people. This position is captured by the statement of America's most prestigious scientific organization, The National Academy of Science: "In a nation whose people depend on scientific progress for their health, economic gains and national security, it is of utmost importance that our students understand science as a system of study, so that by building on past achievements, they can maintain the pace of scientific progress and ensure the continued emergence of result than can benefit mankind." (NAS, 1984 p.6)

The current trend of industrial and economic development in the western countries clearly point to the adherence of the principles advocated by the American National Academy of Science. Some Americans are concerned about the one-directional outlook of economic and social development based on solely science and technology. Sadly their voices do not go far enough and their admonitions about the fact that there is more to life than economics are not heeded. Aleksandr Solzhenitsyn, the Russian writer has commented: 'As creature comforts continue to improve for the average person, so spiritual development grows stagnant. Surfeit brings with it a nagging sadness of heart, as we sense that the whirlpool of pleasures does not bring satisfaction and that before long, it may suffocate us … No, all hope cannot be pinned on science, technology, economic growth. (1995, p.8-9)

The community into which the science for development model has been introduced is one where the people, the Ghanaians, some of whom have had contacts with western culture are still firmly attached to their traditional background. They still practice profound ancestral worship and veneration. The belief is that ancestors offer protection to their descendants and in return are propitiated. This is unacceptable in the western culture whose science is being introduced. The relationship between elders and their juniors is still dependent on the respect for the aged. Children are expected to maintain low profile in the presence of their elders and are not expected to argue with them, since age has an ascribed social status in the Ghanaian community.

One of the main causes for the failure of the science for development concept in Ghana can be deduced from Cobern's statement 'accepting the tight, linear science - technology – economic development (STD) model squeezes out non-scientific ways of knowing and in doing so, creates for science (in its scientific form) a privileged status in society. As this occurs there is increasing pressure for other aspects of culture to conform to scientific thinking. Any areas of resistance come to be viewed as deficiencies because the areas of resistance impede the takeover by scientific rationality'. (Cobern, 1998, p.20-21)

It would be naïve for any one to think that the advocates of science for development in the developing countries would sit down unconcerned to have their efforts thwarted by local practices. They are not only to transfer scientific knowledge but through that impose the western culture on the people. According Basala, the first task pertaining to the subject of world view is that: 'a resistance to science on the bass of philosophical and religious beliefs must be overcome and replaced by positive encouragement of scientific research (Basala, 1967, p.617). This position is further given support by Poole who states: "it is difficult to see how the less advanced societies can achieve the high living standards at which they aim without assimilating large portions of the western conceptual systems, not least those concepts of scientific significance" (Poole, 1968, p.57). In his book '*The Stages of Economic Growth*', Rostow (1971) discouraged the use of an indigenous scientific enterprise from the scratch when according to him, it was much easier to import a highly ready made and advanced body of scientific knowledge from abroad. The question to be answered is 'For whom would that knowledge be used, to whose benefit and for what purpose?'. Acceptance of this philosophy would only end up in making neo-colonialist states of these non-scientific developing countries. This exactly is the hidden agenda of the science for development concept and was to be a prelude to the current globalization movement.

The culture of western school science or world view is described by Cobern as "scientistic and one which alienates many students" (Cobern, 1998, p.19). Based on the logico-structuralism model devised by Kearney (1984, p.106), Cobern describes descriptors of the seven categories that comprise a world. The descriptors were arrived at from extensive research and examination of the cultural form in which western science is embedded and compares them with the descriptors based on non-western world views. Cobern rightly deduced that the western scientific view of the world as presented in the classroom is often materialistic, reductionist and exploitive (Cobern, 1998, p.19).

These descriptions are explicit in the traditional western dominance them about which a Japanese observer comments: 'in the western idea, man was not an ordinary part of nature. He was a specially privileged creature, and nature was subordinate to him ... he was the master of the natural world, which was at his disposal to analyse, examine and make use of ...; since the natural world and the whole universe were manifestations of God's creation, the study of it was not only useful but also a highly esteemed endeavour ... Such an outlook provided some of the important religious motivation which fostered the development of modern science in the western world" (Watanabe, 1974, p.280). The Ghanaian's relationship with the 'other' or the 'non-self' is holistic, humanistic, religious and completely in contrast to that of the western world view. According to Ogunniyi, the world view of an African is monistic/vitalistic, while those of the western scientist is irrational/impersonal (Ogunniyi, 1983, p.84). With respect to universal casualty, Okeobukola and Jejede infer that the African's attitude to cause and effect is teleological while it is mechanistic for the for the western scientist; "casualty is seen in terms of volition and not in terms of mechanistic laws. Things do not just happen in the traditional African society; events have a cause, but that cause is seen in personal terms" (Okebukola and Jejede, 1988, p.3). Within the concept of the science for development, the Ghanaian student is expected to be objective and non-personal, which are not part of his/her concerns in the logico-structual model of world view.

A Judeo-Christian attitude, according to Genesis 1: 28 "And God blessed them and God said unto them, be fruitful and multiply and replenish the earth, and subdue it and have dominion over the fish of the sea and over the fowl of the air and over everything that moveth upon the earth" Genesis 1: 28). This is exactly what western science is about and a big difference with the Ghanaian world view.

The western scientist presents his world view as superior to that of the non-scientist and it is this assumed privileged status of the western world view that prompted the Maori intellectual, Linda Smith to write 'it appalls us that the west can desire, extract and claim ownership of our ways of knowing, our imagery, the things we create and produce and then simultaneously reject the people who created, developed those ideas, and seek to deny them further opportunities to be creators of their own culture … (and) deny them the validity of their own knowledge. (Smith 1999, p.1)

It must be realized that the western world view had evolved over many centuries from the 16th to the present and had resulted in the presence materialistic and non-spiritual attitude where power and dominance of nature and other cultures is the goal of development.

Based on the logico-structural model of world view one can identify world views that are different but yet scientifically compatible and acceptable. If this existence of scientific pluralism were acknowledged and accepted, wholesale export of a foreign world view would be discouraged. Hewson (1988, p.317) has recommended that 'rather than continuing to encourage the west to donate scientific knowledge and skills to developing countries, a different approach might usefully be taken. Critical dialogue between the west and the developing countries promote conceptual change of the knowledge bases of both and allow for the emergence of a new type of science that is effective in meeting specific problems at a range of levels in developing countries and possibly in the west as well. (Hewson, 1988, p.317)

This dialogue would have to take into consideration the religious nature of the Ghanaian and therefore take note of what Orzel warns against "Now everywhere is a market. There is nothing which has not become a commodity that can be bought and sold. The market with its impenetrable mechanism, its shrines, banks, production and consumption armies, serve as a god for those who have gone astray from religion". (Orzel, 1992, p. 32)

## ALTERNATIVE STRATEGIES

The need to look at other directions and policies, which take due cognizance of the cultural differences in order to bring real developments to the people of the developing countries is long overdue. In so doing on should not ignore the pervasive efforts of the western sponsored institutions like the World Bank, IMF and their collaborators in various schemes to execute their hidden agendas under the guise if globalization, standardization and homogeneity of science curriculum in primary and secondary schools.

An African proverb has it that 'when lost, it is better to return to a familiar point before rushing on'. The perception that anything indigenous is synonymous with lack of progress and innovation must be vehemently rejected. It is now generally accepted that successful development strategies must have indigenous knowledge as a component in the planning.

Africa presently stands at crossroads in search of a new vision of development aimed at eradicating the preventable diseases, alleviating the poverty and establishing human rights and the promotion of human dignity based on traditional practices and culture. The affluence of globalization should in no way blindfold the political leaders since it is just a minority in the society who are benefiting. It is unfortunate that some aspects of the colonial heritage, in particular the educational system with the science that accompanied it have become an albatross on the necks of governments in most African countries.

## Indigenous Knowledge Factor

Developing from below is for many reasons, amore productive approach than that from above, and an essential ingredient is indigenous knowledge. To incorporate in developmental planning indigenous knowledge: is a courtesy to the people concerned; is an essential first step to successful development; emphasizes human needs and resources rather that material one alone; makes possible the adaptation of technology to local needs; is the most efficient way of using western science 'Research and Development' in developing countries; preserves valuable local knowledge; encourages community self-diagnosis and heightens awareness, leans to a healthy local pride; can use local skills in monitoring and early warning systems; involves the users in feedback system, for example, on crop varieties.

These positive reasons together as against the negative reasons, such as the likelihood of failure using indigenous knowledge-constitute a strong case of incorporating this knowledge in development programs (Brokensha et al. 1980, p.7-80). From their study into indigenous systems of innovation in East Africa, Bertelsen and Muller (2001) point to the existence of two systems of learning in Tanzania, one in the formal sector. They draw attention to the fact that efforts to transfer scientific and technical knowledge from the western industrialized nations to the developing countries without concern for their cultures would fail. Pradhau advices, 'science education, in any country, is certainly a systematic and sustained attempt at communication about nature between a scientific and non-scientific or a partially scientific community and as such it should be particular sensitive to the attitudes and presuppositions of both the scientist and the student (Pradhau, 1967, p.649).

Cobern agrees 'science content is science content, regardless of culture, but not so much with its communication. Communicated science, which includes science education, is embedded in culture' (Cobern, 1998, p.18).

## Knowledge Acquisition In The Formal Sector

In Tanzania it was observed that the euro-centric perception of what knowledge is about is the trust in the formal system of knowledge acquisition. Similar situation can be found in Ghana. Wackerhansen (1999) has identified five 'dogmas' as the basis for knowledge acquisition in the western industrialized countries:

a) knowledge is understood as being explicit in something that is being or can be articulated in linguistic way. Thus knowledge can be externalized in relation to humans. It becomes an object, something than can be moved around, stored, sold or bought;

b) Human qualifications are based on rules that can be described. These rules are based on or developed from rational professional expertise and can be written in a set of regulations;

c) Combining the above two perceptions, professional competence is seen as being generated from explicit knowledge combined with rule-based skill to solve problems in ones professional domain;

d) Possession of relevant data bank knowledge
   related to a profession is required in order
   to become a professional craftsman;

e) The single individual is the subject for
   learning and competence. The one that learns
   is the one who has the competence.

These five 'dogmas' are used to guide the training of craftsmen in the formal sector. With these perceptions, formal training as craftsmen has become institutionalized in an educational system where practical traineeship has gained less and less attention in Tanzania. The informal apprentice system is still around although it is not part of the formal educational system. This situation also prevails in Ghana.

## Knowledge Acquisition In The Formal Indigenous Sector

The knowledge acquired by craftsmen in the informal based on experiential and implicit learning with a high degree of tacit knowledge. Although competence is being developed there is no documentation and there is very little verbalization. In such a system the apprentice learns to produce a range of specialized products and also learns to cooperate with other craftsmen, customers and to move within the community and society as such. The learning that takes place through experience is grounded in a mentor-protégé system for skill transfer (Nsana, 2001). In order to survive in the rural areas and in the towns the craftsmen must depend on an acquired ability to navigate in a culture, social and family networks and settings. In rural setting there exists diversity, complexity and high degree of uncertainty. To survive in this setting, craftsmen must acquire other different skills through different types of informal apprentice systems. They should be capable of more than one craft. This will depend on the quality of the crafts as well as the proportion of basic knowledge and local time and place, knowledge that are required for that particular craftsmanship. The core norms and values are determined according to the basic understanding of how, why and when people in the community act. Learning and education systems development in the informal sector are therefore more about developing the skills and qualifications strictly required for a particular craft. The informal knowledge depends on personal qualifications acquired by the embedded in that person who has learnt the craft.

## THE POTENTIAL FOR DEVELOPMENT

Mobilization of indigenous knowledge and technology are very necessary for social transformation. For example, the technology of the village blacksmiths is extremely labour-demanding, cumbersome and low level productive. But for as long as the agricultural technology is based on relative simple tools there will always be a need for the intimate knowledge of the blacksmiths about the particular crops and soils of the particular local areas. Whether animal drawn ploughs or other implements will be introduced will depend on the ability to have a localized adaptive technological capability and repair capacity. In the Ghanaian community, the technology of the preparation of the local food, kenkey, is very demanding and with low level productivity. Intimate knowledge of the raw material, maize and the use of the locally designed cooking utensils are very important for the trade whose success depends largely on the skills of the kenkey producer.

Admittedly, the application of modern western science and technology for development is showing success in the western countries because of the milieu they are operating. In the present era of globalization, the future of developing countries is in jeopardy as it is very easy to be marginalized and thus left in more poverty, disease and lack of social development if the cultures and practices of the developing countries are replaced by foreign cultures through schemes developed elsewhere and imposed on the poor developing countries.

The experience of the Japanese in not succumbing to the encroachment on their culture by the west through western science for development is an example worthy of emulating. The Japanese accepted that science is a constructed artifact, which must be culturally based. This was their basis for their success. 'Science to them is universal for other people and as such science education must be an interpretation based on the Japanese culture-free interpretation of science or science education. The Japanese accepted that the ideas and methods of western science could adequately be taught in Japanese schools within the traditional Japanese world view of nature, even though the results may appear striking different from the western practice of science education' (Ogawa). Ghanaians have to learn from the Japanese in their border crossing into western science for development. The statement exemplifies the Japanese attitude 'I may wear a western suit, but I have a bamboo heart' the Ghanaian should be taught to say 'I may wear a western suit but I shall retain my neem heart'.( Brown-Acquaye 2001)

## CONCLUSION

The present situation in Africa with regard to development is indeed very bad and has prompted President Thabo Mbeki of South Africa to designate this period as the moment of the African Renaissance in which 'we are our own liberators' (Mbeki, 1999). The South African President elaborates further by saying 'An essential element of the African Renaissance is that we must all take it as our task to encourage her, who carries this laden weight, to rebel, to assert the principality of humanity – the fact that she, n the first instance, is not a beast of burden but a human and an African being' (Mbeki, 1999). In this context science educators and technologists have a major role to play if 'She' is not to be seen as a beast of burden but a human and African being. The call to rebel must be taken seriously. The rebellion must be in the mind first, relieving the mind of considering the number of four wheel drive cars on the road, the number of cellular phones in the system, the number of people with access to the Internet etc. as indices of development. These are all desirable but not necessary in the face of the extent of diseases in the community, lack of good quality potable drinking water, good housing shelters and the unacceptable extent of poor sanitation in the communities in Africa. African scientist must stand up and inform governments that just establishing the structures of western democracy in African do not of necessity lead to the eradication of diseases, provision of good drinking water etc. The amounts spent on the establishments of these structures of western democracy to ensure freedom of speech, rule of law, separation of power etc. with the concomitant provision of fringe benefits for the politicians reveal lack of concern for the ordinary person whose needs are very basic and ordinary. These basic needs are not outside the capabilities of the local scientists and technologists to provide. In Ghana for example the problems associated with food are not in the production but are related to post harvest losses. It is known that a lost research work has been done and documented by the Food Research Institute in Accra. Similarly the innovative craftsmanship displayed by artisans at Suame Magazine in Kumasi should put Ghana way ahead in technological practices to solve basic problems associated with housing, agricultural machines and transport. (Brown-Acquaye,2002) Relying on imports is not a way of 'encouraging her who carries the weighty burden to assert herself' (Mbeki, 1999). According to Rogers; "We cannot change, we cannot move away from what we are, until we thoroughly accept what we are" (1980). What are we now? One may ask. We are very poor, messed up and entangled in preventable diseases, which makes one to wonder whether it is worthwhile to bring forth children, as on the first day of birth, these children become sources of sorrow not happiness.

The pictures of these dying babies become the object of ridicule in the western electronic and print media.

Universities and other tertiary institutions in Africa cannot stay aloof in this fight against poverty, diseases etc. Tema (2002) advocates "Research students imbued with the spirit of contributing knowledge that would help rebuild their countries, would reject the idea of conducting research solely on the basis of the supervisor's agenda. They would have the boldness to present research proposals that ask authentic questions. They would also feel challenged to respond through research statements by researchers who have attempted to compare African and modern western thinking".

Tema continues "African scholar also has to take up the challenge of bringing traditional African knowledge into the classroom and to conduct his or her own critical analysis … African researchers should also take it upon themselves to explicate African beliefs and conceptions, such as those that conflict with modern medicine".

Irzik (1998) is of the conviction that the business of science is to apply the facts about the world from the western perspective, but not to indulge in the values and value judgments. Bulac (1998) challenges the needs for the products of western technology. He asserts that people have lived for centuries without TVs, refrigerators, computers etc. Products which are not necessary for survival are being promoted by western powers to encourage consumerism of their products and indirectly make the developing countries dependent on western economy and technology through neo-colonialism.

There is every indication of hope for the development of the third world countries if the advocates of globalization would appreciate what Irzik admonishes 'that the way to acquire knowledge of the world is not independent from the institutions, practices and discourses that produce it and does change historically'.

This statement is indeed a restatement of Feyerabend's pluralistic relativism that states 'every culture, every nation can build a science that fits its own particular needs' (Fayeraband, 1989). Ogawa (1989) also states 'every culture has its science'. There are as many kinds of science as there are societies which makes it irresponsible and without any grounds for any one to claim a cognitive superiority over the others. The solution lies in recognizing your own and upholding it. There is nothing wrong about learning other worldviews and incorporating the good and acceptable portions into one's own.

Wholesale importation of development plans, devised and drawn within the western worldview will never succeed in any developing country. The indigenous knowledge which is undervalued and which is disappearing needs to be resuscitated and be made the pivocal resource in the search for development. This way is technically the easiest and most convenient. It is up to politicians and their advisors to realize this and accept it. Rome was not built in a day. It if is realized that indigenous knowledge is derived within the immediate context of the livelihoods of the people and as such it is dynamic there would be constant modifications as the needs of the people and society changes.

President Olusegun Obansanjo of Nigeria, in his plenary address of the World Education Forum declared in part 'The global village of the new century cannot afford (for reasons of equity, equality of nations and world security) to have impoverished ghettos in its fringes. It is in fact in the interest of the richer countries to come urgently to the assistance of the poorer ones. The operative word if assistance – that is technical, logistic and financial help in articulating endogenous ideas for development and seeing them to fruition as well as in strengthening individual and institutional capacities.

# CHAPTER THREE:
# IMPACT OF SCIENCE AND TECHNOLOGY AND GLOBALISATION ON DEVELOPMENTS IN THE DEVELOPING COUNTRIES OF AFRICA

## INTRODUCTION:
## THE REALITIES IN THE DEVELOPING COUNTRIES

There are some countries in the world which can be associated with the prevalence of abject poverty, communicable but preventable diseases particularly among infants, poor sanitation, poor housing, lack of adequate health facilities, lack of potable water, poor nutritional status among the people and numerous other unacceptable social and health conditions in the present $21^{st}$.century. The above listed litany of woes is manifested in the relatively low standard of living in these countries These countries are generally referred to as the 'Developing countries' and are mostly found in sub-saharan Africa and in other parts of South East Asia. These countries have relatively underdeveloped industrial bases which culminate in low levels of economic and social developments in terms of education, health care, life expectancy, literacy rates, infant and maternal mortality, high population growth, low incomes and high unemployment. Because of the negative connotations associated with these conditions the use of the term 'Third World' which was previously used to describe these countries has been phased out.

Sources and causes of the underdevelopment status of these countries, in particular those in the sub-saharan African countries can be traced and associated with the following factors and conditions, among others,

1. Culture and attitudes of the people
2. Irresponsible behaviours of the political and community leaders
3. Unacceptable tastes and aptitudes for luxurious and expensive lifestyles mostly among the senior public officials and politicians
4. non-conformity to laid down procedures and rules governing public services
5. neglect for the rule of law
6. nepotistic and tribalistic attitudes of persons in authority
7. corruption among public officials and holders of political appointments
8. high rates of fertility
9. high population growth
10. low investment
11. patronizing attitudes and influences of multilateral organizations such as the World Bank, IMF and their associated organizations, development agencies and some international non-governmental organizations(NGOs) with regards to formulating and executing of policies. These tend to portray them of imperialistic and colonial mentalities in the host countries.

12. influence and selfish interests of multinational
    companies in the host developing countries
13. effects and trends in the globalization processes
    and the international free market economies
14. unprofessional execution of planned
    economic and development activities
15. ad hoc modifications to properly discussed and
    planned activities without due consultations
16. conspicuous show of power by authorities
    towards their subordinates
17. lack of manpower planning and poor
    human resource management.

The interplay of the above situations and conditions create fertile grounds for the perpetuation of the underdevelopment status of the sub-Saharan countries.

In one of these sub-saharan countries a huge dam was built over one of the rivers for the generation of hydroelectric power. Most of the industrial enterprises and domestic consumption of electricity rely on this facility. Over the past years, however the level of the water behind the dam had been allowed to fall below the minimum level for efficient generation of electricity. The fall in water level was occasioned by the unpredictable and erratic rainfall patterns in the country. Effective plans could have been devised to maintain the water level at reasonable operational heights. This was not done and for that reason any time the water level fell low the supply of electricity had to be rationed and thus put industrial companies out of regular operation.

It is very common in some of these sub-saharan countries to hear of a newly appointed chief executive of a public institution, including universities, demanding for the purchase of an expensive saloon car for his/her personal and official use and another one for domestic use.

Relatives and friends of some chief executives in some public institutions may be appointed to posts for which they lack the qualifications and the requisite track professional experience.

Such and similar situations are never heard of in those countries described as developed which have high per capita incomes and associated very high living standards with high Human Development Indexes (HDI) The HDI is a UN categorisation which is used as an indicator for the level of human development based on selected statistics. Developed countries have generally HDI of 0.8 or more. Developing countries have low HDI of between 0.5 and 0.8 and accordingly exhibit moderate or very low development.

It is generally considered that developed countries have high levels of economic development because successful economic enterprises have intrinsic values based on a combination of:

a. personal professional integrity of the management staff
b. presence of and practice of democratic form
   of governance in those countries
c. general lack of corruption in high places
d. abhorrence of practices based on ethnic
   and tribal considerations
e. transparency and accountability in the
   transaction of official businesses.

Historic exploitation of the wealth of most developing countries by their respective colonial administrations had also contributed immensely to the economic underdevelopment of the countries. This factor is however not strong enough to warrant the continuation of the status quo. Interestingly the current involvement of the rich developed countries in the globalization processes is supposed to assist in the development programmes of the developing countries.

The use of the term 'development 'to distinguish between countries has drawn many critics who consider its use inappropriate, as it seems to be more associated with modernization, in particular modern technology, capitalism, economic globalization and industralisation. Attention should be drawn to the fact that modernization may have harmful effects on both human and environment. The critics would want to highlight consideration and references to local traditions and values, religion, spirituality, environmentalism and other cultural practices, which have been the historic mainstay of the communities .

Sustainable development seems to be the preferred term and is often drawn into the equation when describing development. This term is referred to as development that is able to distinguish between economic growth and environmental protection. Economic growth is seen to support biodiversity, to relieve poverty and to utilize natural capital properly without its long-term harmful consequences. The Brundtland Report as presented in "Our Common Future" talks of sustainable development as one which' meets the needs of the present without compromising the ability of future generations to meet their own needs.'

Unfortunately most developing countries in Africa fall short of the demands in the concept of sustainable development as portrayed in the Brundtland Report. Due to intensive human activities the environment is heavily degraded The regular and uncontrolled consumption of nature's resources such as trees, land,water and even air exceed nature 's ability to replenish them. In the process of the so-called development, factors such as overpopulation, excessive use of farm lands, rural drift of people to the urban centers, industralisation, over fishing, lack of regulation to protect the environment and a multiple of others, all play various roles to cause and intensify environmental degradation. Through environmental sustainability, it is very possible to halt or minimize these degradations or even reverse the processes they lead to.

It is very sad to say, however that the visible conditions in the developing countries in Africa leave much to be desired. Poverty stirs at one's face, diseases are everywhere and  disease like malaria is known to kill more children than the dreadful HIV/AIDS claims on adults. Potable water is not available. Nursing mothers who cannot afford to buy hygienic nappies for their babies are forced to use their old used clothes as nappies. Laundry soap is often too expensive for these nursing mothers that they wash the dirty nappies without soap. They also have to buy buckets of water for bathing themselves and their babies. The situations are very alarming and disheartening and call for effective actions to rectify the situations especially in those African countries, which luckily do not face natural disasters.

## SCIENCE AND TECHNOLOGY ON DEVELOPMENT IN THE DEVELOPING COUNTRIES OF AFRICA

The developed countries differ significantly from the  developing countries in their social and economic developments. The differences can be linked to their respective reliance on the use of science and technology in their daily lives. Science and technology are important actors in the life of all countries, regardless of culture and level of material development. These days there are no spheres in living conditions in which science and technology are not involved. In private spheres as citizens, in work environments and also as consumers of the products of science and technology, decisions at the personal as well as the general social and political levels, the presence of the influence of science and technology is felt.

In the developed countries technological progress is associated to the early recognition of a good educational system in which the role of science and technology is emphasized and prioritized. For example, the rapid economic success of Japan cannot be mentioned without the role played by science and technology education. It is paradoxical, however that in spite of the increasing reference to the importance of science and technology education in development, many developing countries particularly in Africa face problems related to lack of students interest in science. This situation is worsened by low government financial support for science education which reflect in lack of appropriate teaching and learning materials, non-existence of properly equipped laboratories, lack of motivation on the part of the science teachers, presence of untrained science teachers. Subjects in science that are supposed to describe the real and concrete world are considered as abstract and irrelevant and are thus either neglected or not properly taught. Students therefore develop hostile and ambivalent attitudes and perspectives towards these subjects. The mastery and utilization of modern science and technology have been identified by Abdus Salem, the 1979 Nobel laureate in physics, as areas that have differentiated the developed countries from those considered developing. In the developed countries, the practical applications of science and technology have produced the environment to put in more emphasis on science and technology. Increasing funding for science research is considered as long-term investment. This position is very different from that pertaining in the developing countries where research institutions are starved of adequate funds for research. In the developed countries universities are encouraged to regard research in the basic and applied sciences as contributing significantly to the long-term social, economic and military security of the countries. The early identification of technical talents in students and the stimulation and nurturing of such students are among the routine assignment for the teachers and the school administration. Science in the developing countries are regarded as marginal activity and according to Abdus Salem, 'governments in most developing countries in sub-saharan Africa do not associate the importance of the use of science and technology to their social and economic developments.' Only lip service is paid to this realization by governments and policy makers. Science policies are even not made and haphazard references to science and technology education are the frequent inferences considering them as panacea for development. Infusion of financial support for research, which involves huge costs, are shunned at and neglected. The governments fail to recognize that barriers to the path of social and economic developments are caused by inadequate scientific infrastructure.

The Chairperson of the Governing Council for Scientific and Industrial Research (CSIR) in Ghana, a developing country in the sub-saharan region, is reported to have told university students that " we are joking as a country until we begin to take science and technology seriously".(Daily Graphic,2005)He was also saddened by the fact that the CSIR used 93% of its annual budget to pay salaries and only 3% was actually spent on research and development. In February 2006, the Ghana Minister for Foreign Affaires was quoted as saying "Ghana's future depends on the accelerated growth of the economy, which is best fed by knowledge particularly in the fields of science and technology". He was speaking to the university students in Tamale. He went on further to add "our future competiveness as a nation and our quest for advanced status are fated for a crash –landing without the major impact of science and technology" He expressed the hope that a pan-African approach to the role of science and technology in development would be more cost-effective and significantly better. With such a pan-African approach the African Union leadership could prioritise the use of science and technology and encourage the break down of the geographical barriers between the continent's scientists.(Daily Graphic 2006)

African governments have not denied the importance of science and technology for development. This point has been echoed by the science academies of the G8 group of the world's most industralised countries (2006).The Network of African Science Academies also realize this and had warned that the African problems will only be overcome if science and technology are made integral part of the solution. The Network stated" without embedding science and technology and innovation in development we fear the ambitions for Africa will fail" (2006)

With these concerns the G8 groups have on many occasions discussed what to do to enhance science and technology capacity on the African continent. Specific actions for strengthening science, engineering and technology capacities are imperative for Africa and also the role of the universities are considered crucial in the exercise, according to the G8 groups. The biggest obstacle identified relate to the inability of the politicians in the developing countries to provide realistic funds for science and technology education. Although the private sectors have often been invited to contribute, the crucial link between industry and the universities have not been articulated and established. It is known that there are more African scientists and engineers working in the United States of America than there are in Africa. Although this situation is an aspect of 'brain drain' it could be looked at from a different angle and considered as a kind of migration that could contribute to the creation and transfer of knowledge and the emergence of a mass of skilled and educated workforce with commercial ties between both sides. The African scientists who due to the harsh conditions in their countries had to travel abroad for greener pastures would have benefited from their overseas stay in gaining more on scientific knowledge which could be ploughed back home as contribution to science and technology's contribution for the development of their respective countries. Even the migration of unskilled people from the developing countries do have some positive rewards as they remit home some of their financial gains for use by their relatives and families.

Since modern science is very pervasive and affects almost every aspect of social and economic life, special attention is needed in national planning in the developing countries for education, research in science and technology. Lack of effective planning and management are the root causes for the marginalisation of science and technology development. (Choi, Ramanathan, Brown-Acquaye,2002). Only a few developing countries can boast to have adopted national policies in science.

## GLOBALISATION AND ITS INFLUENCE ON DEVELOPMENTS IN THE SUB-SAHARAN AFRICAN COUNTRIES

At the beginning of the current 21$^{st}$. century, the processes that have led to enhance globalization are accelerating dramatically and in great heaps with   the end result of being the  closer integration of the world's economies in all spheres of human enterprises across nations. Factors such as advances in technological systems in transport and communications, mass media, computer usages and accessibility are all very much in vogue and expanding. Even the previously cherished centralized planning of national economies in the greater part of the last century, particularly for the developing countries as strategies to alleviate their poverty and disease-ridden situations, have given way to the current deregulation in the practice of national economic policies. Trade expansion is playing a major and critical role in the accelerated development of the developed and industralised countries. Unfortunately this cannot be said for the developing countries in sub-saharan Africa. The IMF (1997 page45) states "globalization refers to the growing economic interdependence of countries worldwide through the increasing volume and variety of cross-border transactions in goods and services and of international capital flows and also through the more rapid and widespread diffusion of technology".

Close study and interpretation of the above quoted definition by the IMF would put the involvement of the sub-saharan African countries out of the picture and out of scope. The interdependence of countries would lead to the bridging of the gap between the rich and the poor countries. This is rather not the case as the gap between the developed industralised countries of Europe and those in the Americas keep on widening at astronomical rates. The economist, Mahbub ul Haq, a Pakistani, had this to say" In country after country, economic growth is being accompanied by rising disparities in personal as well as in regional incomes. In country after country, the masses are complaining that development has not touched their ordinary lives. Very often, economic growth has meant little social justice. It has been accompanied by rising unemployment, worsening social services and increasing absolute and relative poverty." (ul Haq, 1976)

The above descriptors fit very well with the prevailing conditions in the present sub-saharan African countries. The expansion of the global economy is therefore not synonymous with an improvement in the standards of living of the people in the developing countries. Although globalization relies on the deepening of economic integration between countries with the hope that wealth would be created in the countries, it is only in the developed countries and to some extent in some developing countries in South East Asia, that this is realized. The situation is not at all satisfactory, unfortunately, in the developing countries in Africa. The process of globalization elicits interest based on the manifestation in the economic and financial activities of people. An offshoot of globalization is seen to be economic liberalization in particular areas of international trade and finance. Trends in economic liberalization point to the need for 'openness' of the economy. This is a very difficult task to be expected in the developing countries, which have some intrinsic cultural and developmental problems. Development economists often take as necessary factors of integration and globalization. These are considered as the impetuses for the promotion and enhancement of rapid economic growth through the channels of expanded markets, acquisition of new technologies and innovations, greater competition, proper resource allocation, suppression of corrupt practices in public affairs, improvement of basic human rights for the citizens, transparency in the efforts of governments in the raising of the living standards of the people. Unfortunately these laudable and achievable requirements are not issues of serious consideration in the thinking and planning of the policy makers in the developing countries where personal amassing of wealth through corrupt practices at the expense of the welfare of the people is the main preoccupation of political leaders. The IMF (1997, pg 204) advices on "sound economic policies and the structural reforms necessary to allow markets to function properly…"

Though trade liberalization, openness and globalization in principle should be antidotes to underdevelopment and poverty and be the catalysts to accelerated improvement and panacea to the alleviation of the poor living conditions associated with developing countries, the current world economic environment and policies do not promote or auger well for the anticipated development Further marginalisation, decreasing economic growth, worsening poverty, intensification of preventable and communicable diseases,particularly among infants and babies, are what stare the citizens of the sub-saharan developing countries. They are not spared with ethnic clashes and civil wars making their predicaments intolerable. Economic forces run ahead of political responses so that their governments are impotent to regulate markets .The new international economic order is being moved by transnational companies which operate in 'borderless world linked by global production and consumption systems' (Omar,1996). These multinational companies wield immense economic power, control foreign investment in the developing countries and have influence on the allocation of or otherwise of the needed resources for effective participation in the global market places. Playing on the corrupt tendencies of government officials help them have leeway in the control of the system and maintaining of their underdevelopment status. Technology now accompanies capital across borders and makes it feasible to link the most productive technologies with the low-cost labour, which is abundant in the developing countries.

A lot of pervasive factors abound to militate against the improvement in the standard of living in these countries. These factors include remnants of colonial structures and legacy, backward technology, demography, high population growth, rural-urban human drift, extreme harsh geographic and climatic conditions, ethnic and tribal conflicts, poor infrastructure, unplanned government policies and associated mistakes in their implementation, dependence on primary commodity export, hostile external environment, burden of servicing of external debts and psychological dependency syndrome (Ajayi, 2000, Collier and Gunning, 1997, Iyoha, 2001, Sachs and Warner,1997) The servicing of the external debts is an albatross hanging on the necks of these poor countries which alone further implicates the poverty status.

African countries are basically agrarian. It is therefore unacceptable and unpardonable for the governments to neglect or give low priority to agriculture and allow food production to remain below its potential The use of inputs like fertilizers and modern machinery is very limited. Agriculture still remains rain-fed and is a contributory factor to the low productivity. Africa has an abundant arable land, which spans over expansive agro-climatic and agro-economical zones. These should be the basis for diversification of agriculture and presents the favourable conditions for high agricultural potential. The World Bank (2000,p 170) is optimistic and recommends, "Thus, persistent and comprehensive improvement in policies, institutions and public and private investment could accelerate agricultural and rural growth. "It is saddening to realize that African countries still engage mainly in subsistence agriculture, which is vital for the communal life of the people. It is aimed at local food sufficiency but still does not satisfy the total needs of the people due to excessive post harvest loses .The communities are therefore not self – sufficient in food production and food has to be imported using part of the scarce foreign exchange available A country that cannot feed itself cannot be considered to be politically independent. Its fate and progress will be in the hands of its benefactors and adversaries.

# CHAPTER FOUR

# OAU, AU, NEPAD, AND DEVELOPMENT REVIVAL IN AFRICA

## INTRODUCTION

Just after mid-night on March 6, 1957, the Union Jack of great Britain was lowered for the last time and a new flag of Ghana was hoisted. Dr. Kwame Nkrumah, the new head of state of Ghana declared that "the independence of Ghana was meaningless unless it was linked up with the total liberation of the African continent". The drive to free the African continent from colonialism and imperialism has yielded dividends as today African states are politically independent. However, new and serious challenges have come to the fore. Amongst these challenges include the fact that though these African states are politically independent, they remain economically, socially and militarily dependent on former colonial and other imperialistic powers. Dr. Kwame Nkrumah warned against this new threat which he termed new-colonialism and considered it as the last stage of imperialism. It is the present day globalization. Nkrumah advocated for an African

High Command to prevent Africa's internal and external brutalities and brutalization. The present situation in the Darfur Region of Sudan, the crisis in Somalia, Central African Republic, Chad and other independent states of Africa attest to the visionary leadership of Osagyefo Dr. Kwame Nkrumah. These concerns of Nkrumah led him to seriously advocate for the setting up of the Organisation of African Unity. One of the ... of Nkrumah's Pan African philosophy was that "all African peoples, wherever they may be are one and belong to the African nation".

Today Africans are be considered and thought of as a demoted human category. To-day Africa supplies 61% of the world's raw materials to the developed countries and her economies are still being controlled by the developed countries. To-day African's do not run the productive assets of the economies, not the manufacturing, not the mining, not the services and even the agricultural sector, when due to the vast arable lands on the continent, the African nations should have great comparable advantage. Due to the promptings of the new-colonialists most African nations have liberalized their economies to such absurd levels that they import everything from rice to toothpicks, and used clothes including used under-wears. The over 800 million Africans with the world's richest natural resources still remain a demoted human category afflicted with disease, poverty and ignorance, in misery and oppression. Ethnic conflicts and civil wars have become the day to day occupation in most of the African countries. In contrast, the Chinese with a little over one billion people in population, are able to feed themselves and are poised to become the world's leading economic power in 10 to 20 years time. They have managed to emancipate themselves economically and politically through hard work and self-achievement they have dignified themselves in contrast to the self-degradation and self-pity of the Africans.

The drive and efforts underlying the setting up of the Organisation of African Unity were to thwart or prevent the drift to the present day status of most African nations. The Pan-Africanism mandate considers a race without authority and economic power as a race without respect. And thus is the present status of most politically independent African nations. The state of the African race is presently as pathetic and bleak as it ever has been since Europe unleashed itself on Africa and its people over 500 years ago. The central source of the undoing of African and its children can be attributed to "the absence of a credible anchor of a powerful united Africa nation, a racial powerbase serving as odiment of African history, the repository of African traditions and values, the custodian of the interests and security of every member of the race, the fortress of counter vanity strength against anti-African designs and machinations everywhere" (Osafo, K. (2007), Daily Graphic, April 27, 2007, Ghana). The present day average African lack self-confidence and self-reliance and is prepared to prostrate at the least opportunity before alien races for the crumbs from their countries. Today's educated African elite have all betrayed the African cause and have become the principal agents for the oppression of the African masses. They are non-discriminatorily greedy, egoistic, self-centred and have no compassion whatsoever for the African poor and oppressed. The African youth, the strength of the nation and the continent is frustrated and directionless. They have lost confidence in themselves and are always yearning to travel to Europe or the USA to become labourers.

## THE GENESIS OF THE ORGANIZATION OF THE AFRICAN UNITY

With the dedicated intention of ridding the African continent of the vestiges of colonialisation and apartheid, the Heads of state and Government of the independent states organized themselves and formed the Organisation of African Union in 1963. In addition to the main objective of the organization, it was orchestrated to promote unity and solidarity among African States, to coordinate and intensify cooperation for development; to safeguard the sovereignty and territorial integrity of member states and to promote cooperation within the framework of the United Nations. In the search for the realization of the laudable goals of the founding fathers of the Organisation of African Unity (OAU) various initiatives were taken and substantial progress have been made in many areas which include the following.

1. Lagos Plan of Action (LPA) and the Final Act of Lagos. These were taken in 1980 with the aim of incorporating programmes and strategies for self-reliant development among African countries.

2. In 1981 in Nairobi, the African Charter on Human and People's Rights and Grand Bay Declaration and Plan of Action in Human Rights were adopted. These two instruments were meant to promote human and people's rights on the continent. Based on these, the African Human Rights Commission was established and located in Banjul, the Gambia.

3. Following the protracted drought and famine that engulfed most parts of the continent in the 1980 with its subsequent effects on Africa's external indebtedness, an emerging programme was designed in 1985, tagged African's Priority Programme for Economic Recovery (APPER).

4. In their determination to seize the initiative to enable African Governments to determine their own destinies and to address the challenges to peace, democracy and security, there was the OAU Declaration on the Political and Socio-Economic Situation in Africa and the Fundamental changes taking place in the world.

5. The charter on Popular Participation was adopted in 1990. This was to indicate the determination

of the OAU to place the African citizen at the
center of development and decision-making.

6.  Then came the Abuja Treaty in 1991 which established
    the African Economic Community (AEC). The objective
    and rationale for the AEC was the development of an
    African Common Market. The Regional Economic
    Communities (REC) were to act as building blocks. This
    treaty has been in operation since 1994. The African
    Common Market has however not materialized.

7.  Efforts by the OAU towards their determination
    to find solutions to conflicts on the continent to
    promote peace, security and stability in African led to
    the adoption in 2003 of the Mechanism for Conflict
    Prevention, Management and Resolution.

8.  There was the Cairo Agenda for Action in 1995
    – a programme for re-launching Africa's political,
    economic and social development.

9.  A strategy for addressing the continent's External Debt
    Crisis promoted the OAU to initiate the African Common
    Position in Africa's external Debt Crisis in 1997.

10. The decision taken in Algiers in 1999 on Unconstitutional
    changes of Government and the subsequent 2000 Lome
    Declaration on the framework for an OAU Response
    to Unconstitutional changes were clear indication of
    the unacceptance of militarialism on the continent.

11. In 2000 came the Solemn Declaration on the Conference on
    Security, Stability, Development and Cooperation. This led
    to formulating the fundamental principles for the promotion
    of Democracy and Good Governance on the continent.

12. Various other challenges facing the continent have also been addressed. These included the collective action in the protection of the environment, the fight against international terrorism, combating the scourage of the HIV/AIDS pandemic, malaria and tuberculosis and dealing with humanitarian issues such as refugees and displaced persons, landmines, small and light weapons and many other issues.

13. In the year 2000 at the Lome (Togo) Summit the Constitutive Act of the African Union was adopted and thus entered in force in 2001.

14. Following the emergence of the African Union from the OAU evolved the adoption of a programme of the African Union (AU) at the Lusaka Summit in 2001- The New Partnership for Africa's Development (NEPAD).

(Culled from the Official website of the Department of Foreign Affairs, Republic of South Africa – http://www.dfa.gov.za/au.nepad/nepadbrief.htm)

## THE BIRTH OF THE AFRICAN UNION (AU)

For the smooth transformation of the OUA to AU, the OAU assembly in 1999, decided to convene an extraordinary session for the purpose of expediting the process of economic and political integration in the African continent. Four summits were organized prior to the official launching of the African Union. There summits were:

a. The Sirter Extraordinary session in 1999 which decided to establish an African Union.

b. The Lome (Togo) Summit in 2000 adopted the Constitutive Act of the Union.

c. The Lusaka (Zambia) summit in 2001 drew the road map for the implementation of the AU.

d. The Durban (South Africa) Summit in 2002 saw the launching of the AU and the convening of the 1<sup>st</sup> Assembly of the Heads of State of the African Union.

The hardships facing the government of the African continent demanded a new vision from that of the Organisation of African Unity (OAU). This new vision is based on a united and strong Africa and on the need to build a partnership between governments and all segments of civil society, in particular women, youth and the private sector, in order to strengthen solidarity and cohesion amongst the peoples of Africa.

The promotion of peace, security and stability on the continent became the focus and a prerequisite for the implementation of the development and integration agenda of the African Union.

## The Objectives Of The Au

The main objectives of the AU are:

1. To achieve greater unity and solidarity between the African countries and the peoples of Africa.
2. To defend the sovereignty, territorial integrity and independence of its member states.
3. To accelerate the political and socio-economic integration of the continent.
4. To promote and defend African common positions on issues of interest to the continent and its people.

5. To encourage international cooperation, taking due account of the charter of the United Nations and the Universal Declaration of Human Rights.
6. To promote peace, security and stability on the continent.
7. To promote democratic principles and institutions, popular participation and good governance.
8. To promote and protect human and people's rights in accordance with the African Charter on Human and People's Rights and other relevant human rights instruments.
9. To establish the necessary conditions which enable the continent to play its rightful role in the global economy and in international negotiations.
10. To promote sustainable development at the economic, social and cultural levels as well as the integration of African economies.
11. To promote co-operation in all fields of human activity to raise the living standards of African peoples.
12. To co-ordinate and harmonize the policies between the existing and future Regional Economic Communities for the gradual attainment of the Union.
13. To advance the development of the continent by promoting research in all fields, in particular in science and technology.
14. To work with relevant international partners in the eradication of preventable diseases and the promotion of good health on the continent.

## Some main organs of AU

The African Union has

a. The Assembly which is comprised of Heads of State and Government and is the Supreme Organ of the Union.
b. The Executive Council is composed of Ministers or Authorities designated by the Governments Of Member States. This body is responsible to the Assembly.
c. The Commission is comprised of the Chairperson, the Deputy Chairperson, eight (8) Commissioners and Staff members. Each Commission is responsible for a portfolio.
d. The Peace and Solidarity Council (PSC) was proposed by decision AHG/Dec160(xxxvii) of the Summit of Lusaka, July 2001.
e. The Pan-African Parliament. By this structure the full participation of African peoples in governance, development and economic integration of the continent was envisaged. Ratification is still due.
f. The Court of Justice has been proposed and is to be established.

In addition to the main organ of the Union, specialized Technical Committees have been set up to address sectoral issues and are at Ministerial Levels. The following Committees have been set up:

i. The Committee on Rural Economy and Agricultural Matters
ii. The Committee on Monetary and Financial Affairs
iii. The Committee on Trade, Customs and Immigration Matters
iv. The Committee on Industry, Science and Technology, Energy, Natural Resources and Environment
v. The Committee on Transport Communication and Tourism
vi. The Committee on Health, Labour and Social Affairs.

vii. The Committee on Education, Culture
and Human Resources.

The following financial institutions have also been set up.

- The African Central Bank
- The African Montary Fund
- The African Investment Bank

The portfolios of the AU Commission are:

A. Peace and Security (Conflict Prevention, Management
and Resolution and Combating Terrorism).
B. Political Affairs (Human Rights, Democracy, Good
Governance, Electoral Institutions, Civil Society
Organisations, Humanitarian Affairs, Refugees,
Returnees and Internally Displaced Persons).
C. Infrastructure and Energy (Energy, Transport,
Communications, Infrastructure and Tourism)
D. Social Affairs (Health, Children, Drug Control, Population,
Migration, Labour And Employment, Sports and Culture)
E. Human Resources, Science and Technology (Education,
Information Technology Communication, Youth,
Human Resources, Science and Technology)
F. Trade And Industry (Trade, Industry,
Customs And Immigration Matters)
G. Rural Economy and Agriculture (Rural Economy,
Agriculture and Food Security, Livestock, Environment,
Water and Natural Resources and Dessertation)

H. Economic Affairs (Economic Integration,
   Monetary Affairs, Private Sector Development,
   Investment and Resource Mobilization)

(Culled from the Official website of the Department of Foreign
Affairs, Republic of South Africa – http://www.dfa.gov.za/
au.nutshell.htm)

# THE NEW PARTNERSHIP FOR AFRICA'S DEVELOPMENT (NEPAD)

The harsh realities of the escalating poverty levels, the underdevelopment and continued marginalization of Africa, in addition to the negative effects from globalization prompted the Organisation of African Unity (OAU) to mandate five (5) Heads of State comprising Algeria, Egypt, Nigeria, Senegal and South Africa to develop an integrated socio-economic development framework for Africa. The strategic framework that evolved was formally adopted at the 37th summit of the OAU in July 2001.

## Nepad – Any Need For It

A close and thorough study of the:

1. Primary objectives of NEPAD
2. The principles for NEPAD
3. NEPAD's programme of Action, its priority action areas and desired outcomes all point to confusion as to whether NEPAD is necessary. Every point of importance for the socio-economic development of the African continent had been highlighted and emphasized right from the inception of the OAU through its metamorphosis into the African Union

(AU). NEPAD's programme of actions are just duplications of the various aspects of AU's mandate and activities.

Writing in Africa Notes (Nov. Dec. 2003) Institute for African Development, Cornell University, Ithaca NY, George Ngware, categorical dismisses the need for NEPAD. He maintains "NEPAD was not necessary ... the African Economic Community (AEC) objective was to promote economic, social and cultural development and the integration of African economies in order to increase economic self-reliance and promote an endogenous and self-sustained developments". The objectives of the African Economic Community (AEC) therefore have all the ingredients of an economy that is African-inspired, Africa – driven and African-reliant. Because of the importance and relevance of the AEC, the OAU met in Yaoundé in 1996 to shorten the transitional period initially considered to cover thirty four years to twenty years. By this action, AEC's completion period would have been in the year 2016. The unnecessity in the NEPAD's coming is underscored by the fact that the preamble of the present African Union Charter talks of "the need to accelerate the process of IMPLEMENTING the treaty establishing the African Economic Community in order to promote the socio-economic development of Africa." It is therefore not a new name that is needed but for a new impetus, it is not about the failure of AEC, but its rapid implementation. Sub-Saharan African is in a critical predicament but unfortunately the political will for the governments to face the stark realities and promote the noble and laudable objectives of the OAU and now AU seem to be lacking.

Right now in the year 2007 and previous years, the country DR Congo faces the must serious situation where 71% of the people are suffering from hunger. What does the government of the DR Congo do to solve the hunger problems? They rather promote local ethnic conflicts.

Nigeria, who's President Olusegun Obasanjo was one of the architects of NEPAD, is one of those countries in sub-Saharan Africa blessed with energy resources worth GPD of N283139.38mn in 2004 and showing growth of 3.3%. Regardless of this huge revenue, other sectors of the economy, in particular agriculture have been neglected. Nigeria has a population of more than 130 million and the poverty status of the average Nigerian is sad to contemplate. The country has some of the most fertile soils in Africa and spans a wide range of climates from the hot humidity of the south where the cocoa, coffee and oil palm abound to the dry heart and conditions in the north that support cotton, cereals, legumes and livestock.

Following the presidential and state elections in April 2007, the results of which have been described by the White House and the EU observer teams as deeply flawed and not credible, statements by the President Olesegun Obasanjo and the ruling incumbent government are not healthy for the sustenance of a credible democracy. The possibility of ethnic clashes resulting to conflicts cannot be overruled. The looming electoral crisis in Nigerian's 2007 elections stems from Mr. Obasanjo's bid to have his tenure extended but which was defeated.

The UN Relief Coordinators have reported that in the months March and April, 2007 more people had been displaced in Somalia than anywhere else in the world. Local ethnic conflicts still rage in Somalia, where Ethiopian backed government forces battle insurgents in the Somalia's capital, Mogadishu. These insurgents are believed to be a mixture of Islamists and militiamen from the Hawiye clan, the largest in Mogadishu.

Elsewhere on the African continent, the fighting in Sudan's Darfur region has not abated and has led to protests taking place around the world, tagged Global Day for Darfur which involves events taking place in over 35 capitals to mark the fourth anniversary of the conflict. The West-African sub region has also had its fair share of conflicts based on ethnic and religious uprising. The Sierra-Leone, Liberia and La Cote d'Ivoire crisis are still not fully resolved.

Election malpractices, compounded by key dictatorial regimes in Togo, still simmer and have potential of erupting into serious crisis.

The disturbing aspects of the attitudes of African governments and their seemingly neglect or lack of concern for the various declaration of the OAU and AU. There is the Mechanism for Conflict Prevention, Management and Resolution adopted in 1993 as a practical expression of the determination of the African leadership to find solution to conflicts. The behaviour of African governments towards conflicts in their own countries and in other African countries portrays them as non-caring. They hide under the cloak of non-interference in other countries internal affairs.

The promotion of Democracy and Good Governance in the continent are ideals that seem to have been left and forgotten immediately after they were promulgated at the 2000 Summit. Most of the African governments tend to pay lip-service to the noble objectives set by themselves at their various summits and meetings. By their inaction, the African governments keep on attracting cold and snobbish attention from the western industrialized countries to whom they go begging for financial assistance. No wonder conditionality of democracy and good governance are now key requirements for the little support these western countries dish out to the so-called well-behaved Africa-countries. Realizing the low recognition African governments receive from the west, the South African President, Thabo Mbeki had no choice but to admit "we will have to rely on ourselves, our own resources and ours efforts". Ngware (African Notes, Nov. – Dec., 2003) refers to the actions and inertia of African leaders towards NEPAD as evidence to their lack of belief in developmental decisions they take on behalf of Africa. According to Claude Ake (African Notes, Nov. – Dec., 2003) "they (leaders) are saddled with a strategy that hardly any of them condemn. Lacking faith in what they are doing and caught between their own interests, the demands of their external patrons and their constituents, African leaders tend to be ambivalent, confused, prone to marginalize development and even their role in its pursuit".

According to Ngware, instead of implementing innovative and inward-oriented strategies of development like the AEC, African leaders choose to pursue the policies prescribed by the International Monetary Fund (IMF), World Bank and World Trade Organisation (WTO). Joseph Stiglits, a former chief economist of the World Bank, sarcastically points out that "countries that have succeeded in the recent past have ignored IMF advice; but those who have failed, have followed it". (African Notes, Feb. 2003)

The Herculean problems facing African governments are most often self-imposed and propagated by lack of holistic vision. On development, the Dag Hammarskjöld Foundation considers it to be endogenous and that it can only come from within society, which defines its total sovereignty, its vision and its strategy and counts first and foremost on its internal strengths and cooperating with societies that share its problems. The United Nations Environmental Programme had indicated that food emergencies were occurring more and more frequently in African in particular and that in Eastern Africa, although drought was the main cause, the agency did not rule out the human factors which were increasingly involved. One wonders why water resources in most African countries cannot be harnessed for use in agriculture. According to the World Resource Institute, working in collaboration with the UN Development Programme, sub-Saharan Africa has some of the world's most abundant renewable water resource bases per national inhabitant. It was also recognized that for the year 2005, sub-Saharan Africa use of water for agriculture at 88% of total withdrawals is regionally the highest on earth. Mali and Sudan are reported to use surface water for agriculture to the extent of 99 and 97% respectively. Why then the food scarcity in these sub-Saharan African countries? Ngware contends that from history it is noted that each time the African continent has proposed endogenous solutions to its problems, industrialized western countries, using the carrot or the stick methods, have succeeded in persuading African leaders into participating in a global political economy where they, the Africa leaders come out as reactive agents, economic slaves and neo-colonized political entities. It is unfortunate that the albatross hanging on the necks of African leaders is their propensity to think that the solution to the crisis-prone African continent have to come from benefactors from the industrialized western countries. Ngware is of the strong conviction that the major agenda of popular economic struggles in Africa should be based on forcing states to further self-centred development and promote regional integration. Waindim (African Notes, Nov. – Dec. 2003) is of the opinion that "for NEPAD to make any sense to the average African, its impact must be felt on the breakfast table". The priorities must therefore be set right to include agriculture, road infrastructure, an African passport, African media, African currency, human development and intra-African trade.

The architects of NEPAD should be considered as just intellectual philosophers without any initiatives for practical implementation of the NEPAD. Africa's development growth is being stunted and NEPAD is not the vaccine to stop the cancerous decay of the African continent.

## EFFECTS OF SUBSISTENCE FARMING

Subsistence farming in Africa often demands more labour than can be fed with the food that farmers produce. It is realized that the human population of the continent has never reached the size that it seems capable of supporting. The International Institute of Tropical Agriculture at Ibadan, Nigeria had reported that Africa remains under-populated even at the end of the second millennium with a population approaching 900million. The food production potential of the continent was yet to be fully exploited. A survey by the Food and

Agriculture Organisation (FAO) of the UN, published a report in 1991 that indicated that only 22% of the land on the continent suitable for agriculture was actually in production pointing to under-utilization of the land for farming such suitable crops as cereals, roots plants, tubers, oil crops, sorghum, cotton and various medicinal plants. In the West African forest belt, yams, oil palm, groundnuts, kola, bambara beans, cowpea are some of the agricultural varieties suited for cultivation in the area. The historian J. Ki-Zerbo had observed "the very vastness of the African continent, with a diluted and therefore readily itinerant population living in a nature at once generous with its fruits and minerals, but cruel with its endemic and epidemic diseases, prevented it (the continent) from reaching the demographic concentration which has almost always been one of the pre-conditions of major quantitative changes in the social, political and economic spheres."

It has been estimated that three hectares of land including fallow was enough to feed a family and produce a surplus in any part of Africa where mixed agriculture could be practiced. The problem however, with it was that the amount of labour required restrained the family's ability to satisfy its needs. In the East African highlands it was estimated that clearing of land for cultivation alone would take up 150 man-days of labour per hectare. In south east Nigeria, the annual round of planting and tending yam crops absorbed an average of 230 persons/day per hectare. Farmers have to spend up to 54% of their labour input to the hard task of clearing weeds. The principle of subsistence agriculture demands that enough food must be produced to sustain the existing workforce. When production fails to support the farming community, the seasonal round becomes a vicious cycle; farmers are weakened by their inability to produce more food and have to keep on struggling to stop the downward spiral.

The wheel and the plough have not been involved in sub-Saharan African subsistence agriculture. These have never been an option simply because feeding the animals would place an unsustainable demand on the food-production system; in addition the soils are difficult to plough and domesticated draught animals are susceptible to endemic diseases.

The environment of sub-Saharan Africa has always been generally hostile and unpredictable. This prompts a highly conservative approach to farming and to the business of making a living. It is a heavy task to sustain existing levels of population. Efforts have to be more geared towards minimizing the risk of failure but not in maximizing returns.

The labour requirements of subsistence agriculture are high; population growth rates have over the years been low in most African countries. Agricultural communities in sub-Saharan Africa are barely large enough to feed themselves, let alone supply labour for other activities.

Viewed in the context of the unpredictable climatic conditions, arduous environmental circumstances and endemic diseases that restrain population growth among agricultural populations in sub-Saharan Africa, the unsustainability of food production and food security have been serious constraints on poverty alleviation. The food deficit that results aggravate the malnutrition situation. Nutritional deficiencies are particularly hard on child-bearing women whose pregnancies inevitably span at least one period when food is scarce and their workload is high.

## Debilitating Diseases

### *Cholera*

This is a disease spread mostly through contaminated water and unsanitary conditions. It  is endemic in sub-Saharan Africa. It is an acute infection of the intestines and is caused by a bacterium of the kind classified as a vibro. Vibro chlolerae and v.ct tor are the species that cause the disease in man. Its main symptom is copious diarrhea.

The vibrios grow well at 25 to 30°C where a population draws its water from a river or canal and consumes this water without further treatment. Contamination with the faeces of a cholera victim makes the water dangerous and put the population at risk. Houseflies which, as adults, are attracted to and feed on human faeces may also spread the vibrios when they subsequently walk over food intended for human consumption. With poor sanitation and lack of sewerage treatment in most African countries, the occurrence of cholera is common place.

## Measles

This is a very infectious, world-wide disease of children. It is very prevalent in developing countries where most of the 777,000 deaths, out of 30 million cases reported by WHO in the year 2001 occurred. In Nigeria, measles is regarded as the most acute infection in children. Those aged $1^1/_2$ to $2^1/_2$ years are most at risk and there is a 5 to 10% death rate. Symptoms include high fever, coughing and a maculo-papular rash. Common complications include diarrhea, pneumonia and ear infections.

## Tuberculosis (TB)

The disease, according to WHO causes nearly 2 million deaths every year. According to the projections by WHO, nearly 1 billion people would be infected between the years 2000 and 2020 if more effective preventive procedures are not adopted. Most of the victims are anticipated to be in sub-Saharan African where the unhygienic environmental conditions make the spread of the disease conducive and easy. Tuberculosis is caused by a very small bacillus, known as Mycobacterium. There are several species of the bacillus and the most commonly causing tuberculosis of the lungs is M.tuberculosis. The disease is spread generally by droplet infection. The bacteria are inhaled and the first lesions or signs of damage to tissues develop in the lungs.

The Centres for Disease Control (CDC) in Atlanta, USA, and the World Health Organisation (WHO) both estimate that approximately half of all deaths caused by infectious diseases each year can be attributed to just three infections, namely Tuberculosis, Malaria and AIDS. These three together accounts for over 300 million illnesses and more than 5 million deaths each year with the majority cases in the developing countries of Africa where many people do not have access to good medical care.

## *Malaria*

This is a mosquito-borne disease that affects 300-500 million people annually, causing between 1 and 3 million deaths. It is most common in tropical and sub-tropical climates and is found in 90 countries. However 90% of all cases reported occur in sub-Saharan Africa. Most of its victims are children. The parasite causing the disease is a microscopic single-celled animal (protozoan) belonging to the genus <u>Plasmodium</u>. It lives in the red blood cells and liver cells of man. Infection is normally the result of being bitten by a female anopheline mosquito that has already sucked blood from a malaria victim and is therefore carrying the parasites. The mosquito thrusts its feeding tube or stylets through the human skin and injects saliva containing an anti-coagulant, a chemical that prevents blood from clothing. Thus it can suck blood freely and also withdraw its stylets after feeding. When an infected mosquito injects saliva into its human host it introduces hundred of spirozoites into the blood stream. These spirozoites are carried around the body in the blood stream but they can develop further only in cells in the liver, where they multiply over a period of about one week. Some remain multiplying over a period while others are released in their thousands into the blood stream where they invade the red blood cells. Inside the red blood cells the parasites feed, grow and again reproduce asexually. This reproduction is completed about 48 hours after the red cells were first invaded and the cells subsequently collapse.

The first attack usually takes place ten to fifteen days after infection and is often preceded by tiredness, aching and sometimes vomiting.

The period is followed by the <u>cold stage</u>, characterized by shivering and chattering of the teeth. This lasts for one to two hours and follows the release of the parasites from the red cells. The disease then enters the next stage – the <u>hot</u> stage after the parasites have quickly entered fresh red blood cells. The patient feels hot with the temperature rising up to 40°C (104°F) or higher. Rapid breathing and pulse rate are observed accompanied by headache and general discomfort for three to four houses. The next stage is the <u>sweating</u> stage during which profuse sweating takes place for between two to four hours. The temperature falls to normal and there is a feeling of relief by the patient. The onset of the next fever may come two or three days later.

In the sub-Saharan African endemic areas, nearly all children are infected by the time they are two years old. Such widespread intensity can be partially explained by the fact that the parasite is carried from host to host by a female mosquitoe that feeds by preference on human rather than animal blood. The devastating and debilitating effect of malaria on the children in sub-Saharan African countries poses great challenges to these African governments.

## *HIV/AIDS*

From many studies, sub-Saharan Africa is considered to be the worst affected area in the world with the most rapid spread of HIV and the AIDS pandemic, causing severe human suffering. From many studies, it has been reported that sub-Saharan Africa is the region of the world that has been worst affected by the AIDS epidemic, causing severe human suffering. Reports indicate that during 2005 alone, an estimated 2 million adults and children died as a result of AIDS in sub-Saharan Africa. It has also been estimated that more than 15 million Africans have died from AIDS since the beginning of the epidemic. Although countries in sub-Saharan Africa have very low GDP, the direct medical costs of AIDS have compounded their financial problems adding an estimated amount of about US$ 30 per year for every person infected. Overall public health spending in most of those countries is less than US$10 per year. Although no part of the population is unaffected by HIV it is often the poorest sectors of society that are most vulnerable to the epidemic and for whom the consequences are most severe. Generally, the presence of AIDS means that the household will dissolve as the results of parents dying and children being sent to relatives for care and upbringing. AIDS strips families of their assets and income-earners, making worse the impoverishing of the poor. It has been further suggested that households where an adult had died of AIDS were four times more likely to dissolve than those where no deaths had occurred. For example, in Botswana it has been estimated that, on average, every income earner was likely to acquire one additional dependent over ten year period due to AIDS epidemic. Similar situation occurs in the sub-Saharan African countries where it is observed that individuals who would otherwise provide a household with income are prevented from working by HIV and AIDS, either because they are ill themselves or because they are caring for another family member who is ill. In such situation, children are forced to abandon their education and in extreme cases women may be forced to become sex workers. A study conducted in Burkina Faso, Rwanda and Uganda has indicated that AIDS will not only reverse progress in poverty reduction, but will increase the percentage of people living in extreme poverty, from 45% in 2000 to 57% in 2015. The AIDS epidemic exacerbates the food insecurity situation in most of the sub-Saharan countries as agricultural work is neglected or abandoned due to household illness. It has been estimated that by 2020, Malawi's agricultural workforce will be 14% smaller than it would have been without HIV and AIDS. Toby Solomon, Commissioner for the Nsanje District in Malawi is reported by Claire Nullis, Associated Press, as saying in October 18, 2005 "Malawi Village Underscores Impact of AIDS", "Our fields are idle because there is nobody to work them. We don't have machinery for farming, we only have manpower – if we are sick, or spend our time looking after family members who are sick, we have no time to spend working in the fields".

As parents and family members became ill, children take on more responsibility in order to earn an income; they have to produce food and care for the sick family members. Adequate nutrition eludes these children. These children miss school as their parents have no money to send them to school. They may be lucky if their grand-parents are in the position to care for them. As the epidemic worsens, the education sector is damaged which in turn is likely to increase the incidence of HIV transmission. Without education AIDS will continue its rampant spread. With AIDS out of control, education will be out of reach", cautions Peter Piot, Director of UNAIDS. A decline in school enrolment is one of the most visible effects of the epidemic. This will in itself have an effect on HIV prevention, as a good basic education ranks among the most effective and cost-effective means of preventing HIV. Studies have revealed that young people with little or no education may be 2.2 times more likely to contact HIV as those who have completed primary education.

The vast majority of people living with HIV in sub-Saharan Africa are between the ages of 15 and 49, the prime period of their working lives. The situation enable AIDS to weaken economic activity by squeezing productivity adding costs, diverting productive resources and depleting schools The combined impact of AIDS – related absenteeism, productivity declines, health-care expenditures could easily cut profits by 6-8%.

As increasing numbers of children are born with HIV due to the fact that their mothers were infected. Life expectancy of the individual is affected. A recent study found that the average life expectancy of individuals living in sub-Saharan Africa has fallen by five years since the early 1990s, mainly because of AIDS. The biggest increase in deaths has been among adults aged between 20 and 29. This group accounts for 60% of all deaths in sub-Saharan African, compared to 20% between

1985 and 1990, when the epidemic was in its early stages. By affecting this age group so heavily, AIDS is affecting the adult who are in their most economically productive years and thus remaining the very people who could be responding to the crisis. AIDS is therefore contributing heavily in the reversal of human development.

The epidemic is showing no signs of diminishing and if this situation is not halted, the people of sub-Saharan Africa will continue to be poorer and poorer. More sobering news refer to a report from the United Nations which projects that AIDS will kill all 15 year olds in Zimbabwe, Botswana and South Africa if no serious actions are undertaken soon. The report goes on to infer that about 24 million people in sub-Saharan Africa are living with HIV. Factors contributing to their unfortunate tragedy include:

## Lack of Funding

To fight the disease and prevent the spread of HIV, funds must be provided. This basic requirement is lacking. Funds for education, testing and counseling are vital for these important preventive efforts. Without HIV education, these poor Africa citizens continue to be in the dark about how they can change behaviors to halt the spread of the disease. The preventive education could include the use of condoms, without which heterosexual transmission would continue to soar. In situations where unprotected sexual contact is common, transmission is more likely and more widespread so that the reported incidence of 1 in 3 adults being infected with HIV in some African countries cannot be disputed.

Due to the lack of widespread testing and counseling, of the 24 million or more with HIV, a large number of them are unaware that they are infected. Hence heterosexual contact becomes a major transmission rate of young adults in Africa. The combination of not knowing their HIV status and the lack of available condoms, allows unprotected sexual transmission to continue.

## Lack of medication

It has been proven that HIV medications do slow the progression from HIV to AIDS. The fight against HIV in the western world has greatly been bolstered by the emergence of HIV medications. Unfortunately those drugs are not readily available in sub-Saharan Africa and thus the people fall prey to AIDS at alarming rates.

## Cultural differences

A big barrier to containing the HIV epidemic is cultural differences that make fighting the disease much more difficult. In some African populations having multiple sexual partners is expected as part of cultural expression. The sheer numbers of sexual contacts, most of which are between parties who are not aware they are infected, increases the risk of transmission. Coupled with this cultural attitude, complacency has also led to a rise in unprotected sex. The complacency rises from the realization of the success of medications which prompt those who can afford to pay for the drugs if infected. This state of mind has may ramifications and some experts project that two thirds of the sub-Saharan population will eventually be wiped out by AIDS. The whole population, a culture and a people are on the devastating attack by AIDS unless something drastic and spontaneous happens.

# EXTERNAL FACTORS

## Natural Resources Exploitation By Outside Speculators

Decision making about the use of natural resources and who benefits from their use, are fundamental to all efforts in alleviating poverty on the African continent. Much of the wealth of the continent stems from its natural resources both agricultural and mineral.

It is generally recognized that the African continent is a rich continent but made poor by the uncontrolled exploitation by the western industrialized countries.

## Africa's Oil Wealth

Algeria, Egypt, Libya, Sudan, Nigeria and Gabon are the major petroleum and natural gas producing countries in Africa. Recently it has been reported that Sao Tome and Principe, a small archipelago on the West African Coast, with a population of 150,000 has become Africa's newest petro-state. The question one is attempting to answer is whether this small country with its newly found oil wealth would join the world's poorest and worst-governed countries on the African continent. Reliable estimates put the amount of oil found in Sao Tome zone to be more than 10bn barrels. Mismanagement of oil revenue in most of the African oil producing countries is common place with disastrous results which keep their citizens in extreme poverty. The neighbours of Sao Tome and Principe, to the east Gabon, whose President, Omar Bongo has been in power for more than 37 years (2007), to the north Nigeria, which has had a history of military coups and been riddled with corruption, these neighbours do not have any good examples of good governance and transparency to show to make outsiders enthusiastic about Sao Tome's ability to escape the so-called curse of oil wealth.

Serious concerns have been expressed about the possibility of a slide towards the kind of oil-related corruption that has been the trade mark over the past decades since the 1970's that has undermines politics and the economic well-being in Nigeria. The people of Sao Tome have been observed to be skeptical about their newly found oil wealth and are heard to be commenting that "it is good for oil to come but we not going to benefit".

In November 1995, a Nigerian activist tried to make poverty history. He, Ken Saro-Wiwa, along with eight other citizens of the Ogoni area in the Niger Delta district of Nigeria, a vast oil region, were all killed by the Nigerian government. Their crime was insisting to get the people of Ogoni region benefit from the oil resources of their area. They also demanded for political decisions to be made in the interest of the people instead of the interest of the western multinational oil corporations, particularly SHELL that had kept the people in desperate poverty. They were sentenced to death by hanging. Their campaigns for better life for their people instead of polluted rivers, charred farmlands, rancid air and crumbling schools resulted in their deaths from the hands of their own government. The Movement for the Survival of the Ogoni People in the Niger Delta province of Nigeria has ever since the death of their compatriots intensified their demands for a fairer share of the oil revenue from their government but all to no avail. Twelve years (2007) after the execution of Ken Sara-Wiwa and compatriots it is observed that 70% of Nigerians still live on less than US$1.00 a day. The multinational oil company, SHELL is still in control of oil in the Niger Delta region and making fantastic profits because of the corrupt arrangements and contracts entered into with the Nigerian Federal Government. Kidnapping of foreign workers in the region is often resorted to by the movement. Although sub-Saharan Africa is the poorest place on earth, it is also considered to be the most profitable investment destination. According to the World Bank's 2003 Global Development Finance report, "sub-Saharan Africa offers the highest returns on foreign direct investment of any region in the world".

Africa is thus kept poor because its investors and its creditors are very unspeakably and shamefully rich.

## Structural Adjustment Programmes (Sap)

The World Bank and the International Monetary Fund (IMF) have for some years past been criticized, for the fact that their programmes have resulted in the worsening poverty in many sub-Saharan African countries. Their Structural Adjustment Programmes (SAPs) have been described as spiralling the poverty situations, although these two institutions have been parading themselves as institutions geared to reducing poverty. Their policies have however been more of propelling increased dependency on the richer countries. The Structural Adjustment Programmes (SAPs) are based on the ideology known as neo-liberalism which are principally concerned with debt repayment and economic restructuring. Unfortunately those poor African countries on whom the SAPs have been implemented have been coerced to reduce spending on those social necessities like health, education and development, while debt repayment and other economic policies have been made the priorities. By the SAP, poor countries have been made to lower the standard of living of their people.

For countries applying for financial assistance, preconditions are applied under the ambit of the neo-liberal economic ideology or agenda which include the following

i. Cut-backs, liberalization of the economy and resource extraction/export-oriented open markets
ii. Minimization of the role of the state
iii. Reduced protection of domestic industries while privatization is encouraged.
iv. Currency devaluation
v. Elimination of subsidies on agriculture and food.

As a consequence of the pre-conditions, the African countries become more dependent on the developed nations and their poverty status is worsened. The following situation can be discerned;

a) The poor countries must export more in order to raise enough money to pay off their debts in a timely manner.
b) The natural resources of these countries become even cheaper and these favour consumers in the developed nations.
c) The African governments need to increase exports just to keep their currencies stable and earn foreign exchange with which to help pay off debts.
d) The African governments must accordingly
   (i)     spend less
   (ii)    reduce consumption
   (iii)   remove or decrease financial regulations

The visible outcome of the implementation of the SAP is the death of millions of children each year. To encourage developing countries to increase their exports poses serious dilemma. As Richard Robbins reports "At first glance it may seem that the growth in development of export goods such as coffee, cotton, sugar and lumber, would be beneficial to the exporting country, since it brings in revenue. In fact it represents a type of exploitation called <u>unequal exchange</u>. A country that exports raw or unprocessed materials may gain currency for their sale, but they lose if they import processed goods. The reason is that processed goods – goods that require additional labour – are more costly. Thus a country that exports lumber but does not have the capacity to process it must then re-import it in the form of finished lumber products, at a cost that is greater than the price it received for the raw product. The country that processes the material gets the added revenue contributed by its labourers" (Richard Robbins, 1999 – Global Problems and the Culture of Capitalism).

Africa Action, an organization working for political, social and economic justice in Africa has been very critical of the SAPs. It reports "the basic assumption behind structural adjustment was that an increased role for the market would bring benefits to both poor and the rich". African Action has been questioning whether the SAPs were appropriate answers to the demands for the corrective reforms African countries desperately needed. The adjustments presented by the World Bank and the IMF did not help build the capacity to recover and did not promote long term development African Action emphasized. According to African Action, the IMF rather encourages the aggressive opening up of countries for trade. It is pre-occupied with too much prioritization and too much deregulations with fewer safety nets to be instituted by the governments. Not all the poor African countries may be as aggressive as the IMF would like, in prioritization and other conditionalities. In deed what most African countries require is essential investments in health, education and infrastructure, before they can compete internationally. The World Bank and the IMF rather demand that the Africa countries reduce state support and protection for social and economic sectors. These African economics are pushed into markets where they are unable to compete with the might of the international private sector. These policies only heighten the poverty situation as they undermine the economic developments. Writing in South End Press, Robin Hanhel in 1999 stated that the IMF has been presenting the same medicine for troubled Third World economies for more than two decades and that those recommendations under the SAF contend on

(a) monetary austerity

(b) fiscal austerity

(c) prioritization and

(d) financial liberation

In order therefore to be considered for IMF support, the African governments had to sign the Structural Adjustment Programme and this action would lead to:

(a) Lending to prevent default on international
    loans that have become due for payment.
(b) Arranging a restructuring of the country's debt
    among private international lenders and which
    would include a pledge for new loans.

(Robin Hanhel 'Panic Rules!', South Press, 1999, pg. 52)

## Natural Resources And Conflicts In Africa

### TABLE 1

### Agricultural and Mineral Resources

| Country | Agriculture | Mineral |
|---------|-------------|---------|
| ALGERIA | Wheat, oats, olives | Petroleum |
| ANGOLA | coffee, bananas, maize | petroleum, diamonds |
| BENIN | coffee, cocoa, yams | Petroleum |
| BOTSWANA | maize, sorghum, livestock | Diamonds |
| BURKINA FASO | groundnuts, cotton, sorghum | manganese, limestone |
| BURUNDI | coffee, cotton, maize | Gold |
| CANEROON | coffee, cocoa, cassava | petroleum, alluminium |

| | | |
|---|---|---|
| CAPE VERDE | bananas, maize, fish | Salt |
| CENTRAL AFRICAN REPUBLIC | cassava, millet, cotton | Diamonds |
| CHAD | cotton, millet, sorghum | Uranium |
| COMOROS | vanilla, copra, bananas, fish | - |
| CONGO (Brazzerville) | rice, groundnuts, maize | petroleum, diamonds |
| CONGO (kingshasa) | cassava, maize, rubber | copper, diamonds, cobalt, gold, zinc |
| COTE D'IVOIRE | coffee, cocoa, timber, maize, rice | petroleum, diamonds, manganese |
| DJIBOUTI | sheep, goats, fruit | petroleum, iron ore, phosphates |
| EGYPT | cotton, rice, maize, fruit | petroleum, iron ore, phosphates |
| EQUATORIAL GUINEA | timber, coffee, rice, yam | Petroleum |
| ERITREA | sorghum, lentils, fish, livestock | gold, potash, zinc |
| ETHIOPIA | coffee, tills, pulses, livestock | gold, copper |
| GABON | cocoa, coffee, oil palm, cassava | petroleum, manganese |
| GAMBIA | groundnuts, millet, sorghum, rice | - |
| GHANA | cocoa, cassava, groundnuts, maize | gold, bauxite, manganese |

| | | |
|---|---|---|
| GUINEA | rice, coffee, pineapples, cassava | bauxite, iron ore, uranium |
| GUINEA-BISSAU | rice, maize, cassava, fish | bauxite, phosphates |
| KENYA | coffee, tea, maize, sugarcane. Livestock | limestone, soda ash, rubies |
| LESOTHO | Sorghum | water, (hydro) |
| LIBERIA | rubber, timber, rice, cassava | iron ore, diamonds |
| LIBYA | wheat, olives, dates | petroleum, gypsum |
| MADAGASCAR | coffee, vanilla, timber | graphite, chromite, coal, bauxite |
| MALAWI | tobacco, tea, maize, cassava | limestone, soda ash, rubies |
| MALI | cotton, livestock, millet, rice | gold, phosphates |
| MAURITANIA | fish, livetsock, millet, rice | iron ore, gypsum, copper |
| MOROCCO | wheat, barley, citrus, dates | phosphates, iron ore, manganese |
| MOZAMBIQUE | cotton, cashew nuts, maize, cassava | coal, titanium |
| NAMIBIA | millet, sorghum, livestock | diamonds, copper, uranium, gold |
| NIGER | cotton, millet, sorghum, cassava | uranium, coal, iron ore |
| NIGERIA | cocoa, groundnuts, palm oil, maize, sorghum | petroleum, tin, columbite, iron ore |
| RWANDA | coffee, tea, sorghum, beans bananas | gold, tin ore |

| | | |
|---|---|---|
| SAOTOME & PRINCIPE | fish, palm kernels, bananas | Petroleum |
| SENEGAL | cotton, groundnuts, sorghum, rice | phosphates, iron ore |
| SEYCHELLES | coconuts, cinnamon, vanilla, cassava | - |
| SIERRA LEONE | rice, coffee, palm kernels | diamonds, bauxite, iron ore |
| SOMALIA | bananas, sorghum, fruits, livestock | Uranium |
| SOUTH AFRICA | maize, wheat, sugar, fruits,livestock, poultry | gold, diamonds, uranium, chromium |
| SUDAN | cotton, sorghum, millet | petroleum, iron ore, copper |
| SWAZILAND | sugar, maize, fruits, timber | asbestos, coal, clay |
| TANZANIA | coffee, tea, cotton, maize, cassava | tin, phosphates, iron ore, diamonds |
| TOGO | coffee, tea, cassava, maize | phosphates, limestone |
| TUNISIA | olives, dates, citrus, wheat | petroleum, phosphates, iron ore |
| UGANDA | coffee, tea, cassava, maize, bananas | copper, cobalt |
| WESTERN SAHARA | fish, livestock | phosphates, iron ore |
| ZAMBIA | maize, sorghum, groundnuts | copper, cobalt, zinc, lead |
| ZIMBABWE | cotton, tobacco, maize, livestock | coal, chromium ore, asbestos |

Study of Table 1 reveals that the African continent has so much natural resources in addition to agricultural resources that it is unthinkable to suggest that sub-Saharan African countries cannot produce enough food to feed their people. The present food situation in most of the countries in Africa relies on importation from the developed countries of such items like, rice, wheat, milk amongst other food items. There is no gainsaying that present day Africa is very poor and the people live in abject poverty, deprived of clean water, lack adequate housing, food, education and primary health care.

Can the chronic perennial poverty on the continent be linked with frequent unending cases of conflicts and civil wars on the continent? Is it that the availability of excess natural and agricultural resources are a doom rather than a bonus to the continent?

Many sub-Saharan African countries are in debt and must make effort to export more in order to raise enough money to pay their debts in a timely manner. Unfortunately the strategy to export more tends to concentrate on cash crops and commodities being engaged in by many other countries, resulting in huge price war. The resources from the poorer countries thus, become even cheaper and increase in the exports becomes the most viable means to earn sufficient foreign exchange for debt payment.

a) The natural resources of these countries become even cheaper and these favour consumers in the developed countries.
b) The African governments need to increase exports to just keep currencies stable and earn foreign exchange with which to pay off debts.
c) The African governments must accordingly spend less, reduce consumption and remove or decrease financial regulations.

Partly due to the price war scenario mentioned earlier, commodity prices tumble. Reliance on the export of few commodities makes the situation more untenable. Ken Lailaw, is reported by Gemini News Service, on Dec. 4 2001, to have said that "more than 50 developing countries depend on three or fewer commodities for over a half of their export earnings. The World Bank reports that in addition twenty countries are dependent on commodities for over 90% of their total foreign exchange earnings."

Oxfam also contends that more than 50% of Africa's export earnings is derived from a single commodity. Numerous countries are thought to be dependent on two commodities for the vast majority of their export earnings; with respect to Africa countries very few commodities are considered.

Celine Tan of the Third World Network elaborates further; "a vast majority of developing countries depend on commodities as a main source of revenue. Primary commodities account for about half of the export revenues of developing countries and many developing countries continue to rely heavily on one or two primary commodities for their export earnings."

In April 2001, the British Newspaper Observer and Guardian carried a report of an interview with Joseph Stiglitz, the former head of World Bank. According to the report the World Bank prescribes "assistance strategies" for every poor nation using careful country by country investigation. According to Joseph Stiglitz, the Bank's investigation involves little more than close inspection of five-star hotels. It concludes with a meeting with a begging finance minister, who is handed a "restructuring agreement" pre-drafted for "voluntary signature". This is the nature of the World Bank; poor African countries have to negotiate with for financial assistance and support!

Ann Pettifer and Joseph Hanlon both consider top-down conditionality as undermining democracy by making elected governments accountable to Washington-based institutions instead of their own people. This situation also has the potential for unaccountability and corruption.

Raj Patel cynically considers structural adjustment policies as weapons of mass destruction. It is generally recognized that every rich western country to-day has developed because in the past their governments deliberately took major responsibility to promote economic growth. A lot of protectionism and intervention of technology transfer were introduced. Provision of some sort of equality, education, health and other services geared towards enhancing the nation were given consideration. These industrialized nations never played down on the role some forms of protection allow capital to remain within the economy and thereby enhance the economy.

It is therefore just criminal for the World Bank and the IMF to use the structural adjustment initiatives and other western imposed policies to coerce the poor developing countries of African to cut back on those very provisions that have helped the developed countries to prosper in the past. One therefore has grounds to ask if development is really the objective of the World Bank, the IMF and their ideological supporters.

Ann-Louise Colgan writing on *Hazardous to Health: The World Bank and IMF in Africa,* in Africa Action April 18, 2002, considers the policies of the two institutions to be impeding Africa's development by undermining Africa's health. According to her, their free marketing perspective has failed to consider health as an integral component of an economic growth and human development strategy. Instead the policies of these institutions have caused a deterioration in health and in health care services across the African continent.

Ann-Louise Colgan recognizes the fact that the goals of the World Bank and the IMF are slightly different. However the policies of both institutions seem to compliment each other. World Bank and IMF adjustment programmes reinforce each other. Using the practice of "cross-conditionality" an African government generally must first be approved by the IMF, before qualifying for an adjustment loan from the World Bank. Their agendas also overlap in the financial sector in particular. Both work to impose fiscal austerity and to eliminate subsidies for workers. The market-oriented perspective of both institutions makes their policy prescriptions complementary.

Africa Action has noted how political interest affect these institutions. According to African Action, over the past decades, the World Bank and the IMF have undermined Africa's health through the policies they have imposed. According to African Action, the dependence of the poor and highly indebted African countries on World Bank and IMF loans have given those two institutions leverage to control economic policy-making in these poor African countries. The policies mandated by the World Bank and the IMF generally have forced the African governments to orient their economies towards greater integration in international markets at the expense of social services and long-term development priorities. They thus have reduced the role of the state and cut back government expenditure.

Basic food security has been seriously undermined. Ann Petifer, head of debt campaign organization, Jubilee Research has reported of the news in 2002 in the UK media of the humiliation the Malawi government had to undergo under IMF directives. The IMF had forced the Malawi government to sell its surplus grain in favour for foreign exchange just before disastrous famine struck. This demand from the IMF was intended to help Malawi repay outstanding debt. The Malawian government had no choice but to comply although 7 million of its total population of 11 million were severely short of food. Ann Petifer further commented that because Malawi was indebted, her economic policies were effectively determined by her creditors, represented by the IMF. There was an occasion that the IMF withheld $47million in aid to Malawi because the Malawi government had exceeded the budget the foreign creditors had set. On another occasion, for "being off track", the IMF also suspended the debt service relief for which the government had successfully negotiated.

As an IMF requirement, the Malawi government had had to remove all farming and food subsidies to enable the market to determine demand and supply for food. This uncharitable and wicked directive caused many people in Malawi to go hungry as food prices rose. The action is uncharitable in the sense that the western rich countries subsidize their agriculture heavily with billions of dollars.

The extent to which most western rich countries use aid for developing countries sanctions go beyond rationality. The Guardian Newspaper of the UK reported in August 29, 2005, how 700,000 about US$400,000.00 of £3million in British and to Malawi was misspent on US firms hotel and meal bills. The Guardian further reported that even notebooks and pens were flown in from Washington rather than purchased locally.

From all indications, the structural adjustment policies seem to have far-reaching consequences than appears on paper. Yet these are some of the mechanisms whereby inequality and poverty has been structured into laws and institutions for most of the poor-sub-Saharan countries. It must be remembered that these policies are being imposed on poor countries as a condition of debt cancellation, debt rescheduling and aid. It must also be remembered that these are being imposed in the names of "good governance", "sound policies" and "poverty reduction".

## AFRICAN UNION – QUO VADIES?

From 1st to 3rd July 2007, Ghana was agog with excitement and expectation at the holding of the 9th Ordinary Session of the Assembly of the African Union in Accra, the capital of Ghana.

Ghanaians, in every walk of life were overcome with joy on this occasion because on Ghana's Independence Day in 1957, the founding President, Dr. Kwame Nkrumah made a pretentious statement in

Accra, the capital of Ghana the same venue of the African Union Summit, that "the independence of Ghana is meaningless unless it is linked with the total liberation of Africa". With that statement Dr. Kwame Nkrumah had linked his country's destiny irrevocably to that of the continent. Ever since that declaration through his writings and on numerous platforms around the world, his chosen recurring theme was "Africa must unite!"

This visionary stand of Kwame Nkrumah was given support by his illustrious colleagues including Emperor Haille Sellassie of Ethiopia; King Mohammed V of Morocco; Presidents William Tubman of Liberia; Julius Nyerere of Tanzania; Jomo Kenyatta of Kenya, Sekou Toure of Guinea; Modibo Keita of Mali; Gamel Nasser of Egypt and some others. The foundation for continental unity was accordingly established in Addis Ababa in 1963 and named the Organisation of Africa Unity (OAU) which is the predecessor of current African Union.

On the 50th anniversary of the independence of Ghana, this subject of continental government has surfaced and returned to the agenda of the summit of the Africa Union as its sole item for deliberation at no other place but Accra, the capital of Ghana.

Although the continental union government was the driving force behind the formation of the Organisation of African Unity (OAU), the idea died down temporary and was revived at the African Union meeting in Lome, Togo in 2000 with many African leaders calling for a continental executive. At a subsequent African Union summit in Abuja, Nigeria in January 2005, the Authority of the Heads of State and Governments of the African Union appointed a Committee to investigate the desirability and feasibility of appointing ministers for certain portfolios for the African Union (AU). However, the committee, under the Chairmanship of Yoweri Museveni, President of Uganda, went beyond its original mandate to propose the foundation of a union government in Africa. The proposal was studied at the AU Summit in

Sorte, Libya in July 2005, after which the AU set up another committee of Heads of State, led by President Olusegun Obasanjo of Nigeria, the then Chairman of the AU Assembly, to investigate the feasibility of the proposal.

Based on a document submitted by the Committee, at its meeting in November 2006, the Executive Council of the AU recognized that the formation of a Union Government for Africa was a desirable goal but expressed divergent opinions about the nature and timetable of that government. It was realized that with the emergence of globalization no single African country would be able to develop and withstand the pressures of the world economy on its own. The Organisation of African Unity (OAU) has always been a loose association of African states and has been a compromise solution to call for a United States of Africa, which was to be both political and economic entity. For four decades African leaders have been talking about the need to form a Union Government. A renowned Nigerian economist and politician, Sam Ikoku had predicted at the inception of the Organisation of African Unity (OAU) that "The OAU, as it is presently constituted will never allow us to achieve African political Union. And because it cannot evolve in this direction, it will degenerate into an organism for protecting the existing regimes in various African countries". As predicted the OAU turned out to be no more than a trade union of ruthless, tyrannical, incompetent African leaders, totally inadequate for solving Africa's massive problems. The road to cooperation has come to an end culminating in bickering and conflict between African states, leaving African politics to be dominated by outside pavers like France, the UK and the USA. African people are now caught in an oppressive international system in which a collection of greedy rulers preside over the rape and exploitation of African people for the benefit of outside powers.

Four decades after the first talk of the formation of African Union, Africa leaders came to the Accra Summit and continued talking about it. The African leaders that had assembled in Accra saw that the majority of them did not want a Union Government now. In welcoming his colleagues Heads of State and Governments of Africa to the Ninth Ordinary Session of the Assembly of the African Union in Accra, Ghana, the President of Ghana, J. A. Kuffour, and the Chairman of AU, reiterated the decisions at the meeting in Addis Ababa in January 2007 that the Accra Summit would be devoted exclusively to the Grand Debate on the Union Government of Africa. President Kuffour reminded the audience that the question of unification was not in doubt and this position was confirmed by the many resolutions and declarations made by the leadership of the continent since the inception of the OAU to date. According to President Kuffour, what remained was the forming of government, and how and when to attain it. The summit in Accra was therefore to concentrate on the content of the Grand Debate. Mr. Alpha Oumar Konare, a former President of Mali and current Chairman of the African Union Commission did not mice words when he set a radical tone for the Grand Debate in Accra for calling for a union government for Africa without any delay. He debunked the prescription of the moderates in Africa who were agitating for a gradual approach towards continental integration. According to Mr. Konare, Africa had wasted too much time on the issur of unity and reminded the meeting that the gradualist approach began some 50 years ago. The questions being asked today, to him, were the same questions asked 50 years ago. Mr. Konare affirmed that all the institutions and protocols needed to push the union government agenda forward were already in place and that what was needed was the political will of the African leaders.

In his opening address to the Accra Summit, President Kuffour of Ghana lamented the poor state of the continent. According to him, the African continent was second to none with respect to natural resources. Nevertheless, the continent has been described in many unsavory terms including "the last frontier for economic and social development" and "a scar on the conscience of humanity". He further elaborated that over the centuries, Africa has suffered harsh and diverse acts of inhumanity, many a time self-perpetrated, but more often than not, from outside borders. To him unwarranted external interventions and political manipulations were at the base of the causes of Africa's dysfunction. President Kuffour however was candid enough to admit that those decades gone by from the inception of the OAU to the formation of the AU were marked by bad governance and impunity in most of the African nations. To overturn events, the current crop of leaders of Africa had decided to create the African Union and also adopt the New Partnership for Africa's Development. According to the President of Ghana, in order to overcome the mountain of political and economic emancipation through integration, the African leaders passed the Constitutive Act of the African Union in Sirte, Libya in 1999, thus establishing the legal framework for the realization of the vision of the union government. Through NEPAD which the African Union adopted as its development paradigm in Maputo in 2002, the renaissance of the continent was also formally declared, so hoped President Kuffour. President Kuffour must therefore have been greatly disappointed when the scheduled meeting of NEPAD Heads of State and Government Implementation Committee could not take place due to late arrival of the delegates. The Heads of State and Government Implementation Committee (HSIC) comprises 3 states per AU region as mandated and ratified by the AU Summit of July 2002 and is the highest authority of NEPAD. The HSIC reports to the AU Summit on an annual basis. How serious is the HSIC if the delegates or members failed to arrive in Accra early enough to meet and to report to the Summit.

Who should take NEPAD seriously? Who should take the AU seriously if the various sub-regional groupings that have been perceived as the critical building blocks for the integration process, taking into account the fact that their coordination and streamlining to service the central institutions of the African Union are the pre-requisites for unification, have over the past two decades or so of their establishment failed to perform to the degree of efficiency and purposefulness which would assure the people of Africa that the day of the attainment of the Continental Government is at hand. There are fourteen Regional Groupings or Regional Economic Communities (RECs) and if at the time of the Accra Summit in 2007, the nature of the relationship between the AU and the RECs have not been established, how can the relationship by rationalized to service the African Union, the debate of which was the main agenda for the Accra Summit. Even the conflicts in Africa, the Darfur, Somalia, La Cote d'Ivoire were not on the agenda for the Accra Summit. For whatever reason and purpose, the impression was created that the continent was not ready or able to come to grips with the challenge of designing the sort of government that Africa's integration will dictate pragmatically and when to establish it. This impression must have been successfully created and enforced by the detractors of the African Union. Among the 52 Heads of State and Governments who had assembled in Accra there were those who articulated that the continent had spent the past 40 years sitting on their butts talking and talking about Dr. Kwame Nkrumah's dream of a United Africa, without taking any practical steps toward a continental union. This group of radical Heads of State was led by Mumar Qathafi of Libya. They demanded for the immediate establishment of the Union Government for Africa. Their radical position was firmly supported by their knowledge of the work of consultants who had previously been tasked to look into the feasibility of a Union Government prior to the Accra Summit. The consultants had presented a nine year (2006-2015) plan to integrate Africa into one political and economic entity. This plan was elastic enough to be stretched to 12 years if more time was needed for its implementation. Phase one of the plan was supposed to include changing the nature of institutions within the AU.

Phase two included creating new institutions, including an African Central Bank and changing the Pan African Parliament from a non-legislative one into a body that could make laws applicable over the length and breath of the continent and which was truly representative of the different member states. Phase three was to end the preparations and ensure the establishment of the Union Government. It was argued that sovereignty was not an issue at state since most African states were not really sovereign in the real sense, having lost it to the IMF, World Bank, the USA and France. What kind of sovereignty existed, that it was quizzed when rebels control parts of Sudan, Somalia, Ivory Coast and DR Congo.

That wrong impression was propagated by the co-called leaders who championed for a gradual move towards the Union Government. These leaders lacked the political will. Their stand was deliberate because they had come to Accra to protect themselves from the anger of their people at home who would have said a completely different thing, had a referendum be held on the issue in their respective countries.

In his address at the opening of the Summit in Accra, the host President, J. A. Kuffour reminded the assembly of Heads of State and Governments that it had been agreed that this all important issue of Union Government should be debated upon within the various countries by their respective citizenry so that the views put forward by the leaders would reflect the views of the people. The contributions of the leaders would then be seen as human-centred and owned by the people. According to President Kuffour, it was only the people's ownership of the Grand Debate that would give the Conference its legitimacy and sustainability. This involvement with the citizenry did not happen in most African countries. The so-called moderates fell into two categories, one wanted a continentally coordinated integration of the various regional economic groupings which would subsequently further integrate into the whole desired union.

The other wanted the proposed union to progress steadily with a few member states at a time, beginning with those states which have relatively stronger national economies and greater political stability. This latter group was championed by the President of Senegal, Abdoulaye Wade, while the former group seemed to have included President Thabo Mbeki of South Africa.

A surprising stand was mooted by the President of Uganda, Yoweri Museveni, a darling of the western countries. He raised doubt about the political compatibility of African states – he insisted that due to the fairly marked differences in the political orientation among the states, it was politically incompatible for the states to come together and would be the source of friction and tension instead of integration. He was therefore not prepared to sacrifice his nationality for the global union government. From his stand one could deduce that Moseveni was determined to defeat the rebels in his country Uganda, the Lord Resistance Army. This declaration could have been made in Kampala without him coming to the Accra Summit to portray the typical arrogance of the African leader. Extending the argument further one would question the need for the AU 9th Summit in Accra in July 2007 when the African Union owed US$106.8 million in dues and other financial commitments. This situation implies that many African governments are in economically dire straits. Who bank-rolled the AU Accra Summit? The western industrialized countries still keen to have influence in Africa, or one or more of the radical African governments who see the opportunity to formation of African Union now or never?

Consideration of the provision of the basic needs of most of the people of Africa – which include food, water, health facilities, education, security, electricity is enough justification for the holding of the AU Summit. The provision of these needs constitutes the rationale for government and so it must evolve into the practice of the Union Government when realized.

The Accra AU Summit ended after two days of intense debate. The African heads of State appeared deadlocked, unable to reach an accord on the speed and form of a continental union government. As if tele-guided to resort to the previous experiences in earlier summits and meetings a committee was formed and tasked to draft a compromise communiqué.

The economic and political benefits for the Union Government for African have been deliberated upon in many fora to warrant the AU Summit in Accra, the Grand Debate, which should have been devoted to the formation of the Union Government for Africa.

What happened in Accra, Ghana from July 01 to 03, 2007 has not augured well for the poor, struggling masses of the continent, Africa. Posterity will figure out those who have consistently kept the African poor and without any hope of survival in this era of globalization.

The summit which raised the hopes of many citizens of Africa yearning for integration ended without agreement on a firm timetable on the establishment of a government for the continent. A deep division emerged among the African leaders attending the summit. Despite agreement on creating what was considered to be United States of Africa, the summit exposed major differences over the desired pace of change. Moamer Gaddafi of Libya proposed for the union government, complete with a foreign and defence minister, to be established without further delay. Such a stance by the Libyan leader received disapproval by some other leaders who considered that integration would best be achieved by first concentrating on regional cooperation.

The Summit ended by proposing the commissioning of four studies the results of which would be presented to a committee of Heads of States who would make appropriate recommendations to the next ordinary session of the assembly in January 2008.

The proposed studies would focus on;

a) The contents of the Union Government concept
and its relations with national governments.
b) Examining government's domains of competence and the
impact of its establishment on sovereignty of states
c) Elaboration of a road map
d) Funding of the whole project

The possibility of initiating a fast track process with a select group of mainly West African States was at one stage suggested to have been the brain child of Senegalese President, Abdoulaye Wade, an ally of Moama Gaddafi of Libya.

The vision of having a United States of Africa was still cherished.

But how can it be realized and achieved when there are Heads of Governments in Africa who think that the presidency belongs to them and would do all to retain the post.

On January 15,2008, the people of the republic of Kenya went to the polls to elect parliamentary candidates and the President. The results of the presidential polls were declared by most international observers including the observers from the African Union and the European Union as being far from acceptable international standards and not free and fair. Even the manner in which the results were declared and the winner sworn in as the new President within less than an hour after the declaration left much to be desired. The opposition parties refused to accept the results and more than 600 Kenyans lost their lives in the political violence that ensued.

Just about the same time the ruling government in the Republic of the Cameroon was attempting to change the constitution to allow the President to contest for a third term in office This action led to political tension and instability in the country.

What is the future for Africa?

### AFRICAN UNION!! QUO VADIES.?

# TOWARDS BRIGHTER FUTURE—TASKS AHEAD

In order for the sub-Saharan developing African countries to lift themselves from their present unacceptable conditions and situations which are characterized by abject poverty, poor sanitation, myriads of preventable diseases, high population growth, lack of adequate health facilities, poor basic education and others, strong and visionary political leadership is needed. A leadership that can stand up to the traditional system of doing things and face the challenge of the eradication of corruption in high places; a leadership that can decide on what to accept from foreign donors especially in aid related loans and be bold to reject some of the loans and grants if these are not within the priorities decided upon by the recipient governments. A leadership that will rely more on internally generated revenue for its developmental projects based on well planned and articulated policies. The assistance from donor development partners would not be rejected but would be considered only if they are expressed in the interest of the people without any hidden agenda. Internal projects should be developed by the governments themselves without their being imposed from outside by donor agencies like the World Bank, the IMF and other international donor agencies and governments and some agencies of the UN. The type of leadership being advocated may incur the criticism and wrath of some foreign governments which may label these progressive governments as dictatorial, non-democratic, and go to the extent of passing judgments on them and refusing them assistance unless the conditionalities attached to their offers are accepted. This visionary leadership being advocated would do well to view the African Union as the best venue to help in the solution to the problems facing the African governments. Effective involvement in the activities of the African Union and the NEPAD should be the cornerstone for the policies of these developing nations and cooperation and collaboration with sister African countries would dominate the foreign policies.

This visionary leadership should be strong and bold enough to seriously discuss and decide on whether the benefits associated with the granting of aid under the Millennium Challenge Accounts of the USA government are indeed in the interest of the people in his nation The recipient African countries should have the right to decide on what to use the aids for based on their own selected areas of priority.

Recognition of the role of science and technology in development should gear the countries to adopt well-planned strategies towards the alleviation of their poor conditions. Incorporation of indigenous knowledge systems in school science courses would do well not to alienate the students from modern western science. Because of the inadequate perceptions of science and science learning, there is a disjunction between school learning and local knowledge( Peatcot,1995, Knamiller, 1989). These misconceptions have led to the presence of gaps between the traditional ideas of skill learning among children in the rural areas and adults. These gaps also occur between the national aspirations of curricula of government and training institutions. . Anglo-American models of education are still viewed as the yardstick for quality education. Knaimiller(1982:2) asserts that this is "because we often fail to take into account the science and technology local people are doing, what knowledge and skills they have and what problems they feel are important to consider "Using indigenous technology as a basis for education would boost the retention rate of students in sciences courses It would need the re-orientation in the subjects, teachers attitudes and in all school experiences. Identification of indigenous knowledge needed to be incorporated into the units of subject matter already being taught in the schools should be a matter of priority. Taking into consideration the relevant experiences of the school children, the subject matter has to be presented in such a way to connect logically the factual elements and their corresponding indigenous knowledge.

There are many instances where local knowledge and concepts in school science interact and these should be identified and used accordingly. Current educational practices must take cognizance of new concepts of knowledge that are inclusive of both international and indigenous knowledge systems. As Nyerere (1967) maintained "education must be conceived as the transmission from one generation to the next of the 'accumulated wisdom and knowledge of society," and the preparation of the young for their future membership of society and their effective participation in its maintenance and development. Hence knowledge must of necessity be both international and indigenous. With this admonition from Nyerere and the recognition of the existence of the current effects and influence of globalization and liberalization of world trade in development, developing countries have to gear themselves towards a reorientation that helps them to embrace globalization with all its challenges and uncertainties. There can be no choice, as failure to adapt would mean risking further marginalisation in world economic affairs. The existence and utilization of the information highway by which means the developed countries are able to exchange newly acquired scientific knowledge and technology make it extremely difficult for the developing countries to catch up on technological developments. The scientific and technological infrastructure for the maximum utilization of the information highway is not available in the developing countries. Even the basic requirements of regular and constant supply of electricity and water are hard to come by much less the scientific knowledge developed by the local scientists to feed the highway system. The scope of scientific research being conducted in these developing countries are so basic and no more of international technological relevance that their inputs onto the highway is laughable and looked down upon. Through the use of the information highway developed countries can reduce the differences between their technologies and thereby bring together the integration of world markets for highly skilled individuals. The skills of a good medical officer or engineer are portable across the globe. As an area for the economic development of the developing countries, consideration could be given to the development of a national science and technology policy that would identify and nurture potentially good scientific students in specific science disciplines and train them well enough to be traded on the world market. This practice is being done in some professional sports like soccer, tennis, and football, golf. Governments could negotiate with the contractors of this skilled national manpower and derive financial benefits, which could be used for developments. Countries like China, India Pakistan and South Korea are sending some of their highly skilled nationals to the developed countries on government-to-government arrangements for mutual benefits of both countries. Brain drain on the part of the developing country could be considered as a planned economic asset Highly qualified doctors and nurses are leaving Ghana in large numbers to pursue careers in the USA and Britain and these have proved disastrous for the health services in the home country, Ghana.

With these rapid improvements in communication techniques these Ghanaian migrants can help their home country even when remaining abroad. This can be done by maintaining links with hospitals, industry and research at home. This is an aspect of what has come to be known as 'scientific Diasporas' and could be viewed more as "gain" than "drain".

Ogunsola (2005) opines that the information revolution and the corresponding increase in the spread of knowledge have resulted in the birth of a new era —one of knowledge and information, which affects directly economic, social cultural and political activities of all regions of the world including Africa. Transforming economies into information and knowledge economy are now in practice especially in the USA, Canada and the EU. Some Asian countries like Malayasia,India South Korea, Japan and some Latin American countries like Brasil, Chile Venezuela and Mexico have not been left out of the trend towards the use of comprehensive Information and Communication

Technology (ICT). These countries see the utilization of ITCs as deployments for socio-economic development through which to establish global dominance and reap the tremendous payoffs in terms of wealth creation and the generation of high quality and highly skilled manpower. Through the practice of ICT (Faye 2000), it is possible for developing countries to leapfrog the industralisation stage and transform their economies into high-level information economies. Developing countries need to be encouraged to take advantage of the opportunities that ICTs create and offer. Clear and well-planned policies are what are needed to embark on for economic development. ICTs are being used to produce, access, adapt and apply information for a knowledge economy (Morale-Gomez and Melesse 1998). Many developing countries face the problem of limited scale in the use of ICTs and this raises doubts about their ability to participate in the current ICT –induced global knowledge economy. Despite the undoubted benefits associated with ICTs significant barriers to their effective use do exist in both the developed and developing countries. Some of these barriers are endemic and relate to the generation gap, learning processes and gaining experiences in ICT. Developing countries are faced with the extra problems of poor telecommunication infrastructure, poor computer and general literacy, regulatory inadequacy, technological gaps, erratic supply of electricity and poor governance mainly due to adoption of western style democracy in an environment of very high illiteracy and adulation of public office holders.

With the advent of the dreadful HIV/AIDS epidemic spreading through the sub-saharan African countries, the need for realistic approaches to reverse the current underdevelopment trends is vital and paramount. International cooperation may assist but everything finally rests with the people and their governments if these countries will not be heading to the extinction of their people. The prognosis is very bleak, as the developed world is not going to wait for these countries to catch up.

## POSTLUDE

The current fast lane tracking of the globalization programme for the integration of world economies demands that the developing countries have to evolve very innovative plans and approaches to survive in the system.

One innovative approach is to capitalize on the migration of their own citizens to the developed countries to seek for greener pastures. They are going on their own through very difficult and trying conditions.

Because of the reality of the situation in the USA with the illegal immigration from neighbour Mexico, the USA government has gone ahead to create the Department of Homeland Security. Provision of cheap unskilled labour by the illegal immigrants from Mexico for the agriculture plantations, for the expanding construction industries and in other areas which the average unskilled American high school dropout is not willing to be engaged in is the attractive force for the American employers of these cheap Mexican illegal immigrants. The jobs are there to be filled. Developing countries can save the Department of Homeland Security a great amount of problems if the USA industries that need semi-skilled and unskilled labour force would be encouraged to recruit from far away sub-Saharan African countries where this labour force is in abundance. Since these recruitments would be done with the approval of the governments in the developing countries, an aspect of the globalization process in creating one global village in which the free movement of goods and people would have been achieved. The Department of Homeland Security can then concentrate its efforts on the battle against illegal trafficking of narcotic drugs from across the Mexican border to the USA Hopefully with the passage into bill of the Guest Worker Program in the USA, recruitment of unskilled labour from developing African countries would be done in the open with their governments approval and involvement.

International cooperation would be assured and the prospect of the citizens of the developing countries becoming poorer, with widening poor sanitation and diseases and associated ills in the societies would be discussed in open for a and solutions found. The one global village concept would ensure that the world becomes safe and secure for all peoples irrespective of the continents they originate from. Movements of legitimate goods across borders would be guaranteed and science and technological developments would play their vital roles in the raising of living standards throughout the world.

Similar bilateral agreements between African governments and governments of the European Union can be made for the recruitment of unskilled and semi-skilled labour from Africa.

Just as specific high quality grades of agricultural produce are in high demand in the USA and the EU,the human recruitment should be seen in the general globalization process.

Any assistance from the western industralised countries to help the Sub-Saharan African countries relieve themselves of the qualification "HIGHLY INDEBTED POOR COUNTRY (HPIC) would be most welcome and hailed. Africa needs urgent assistance in the area of development.

In the area of science and technology for development, the inconsistencies and lack of appreciation of the values of the people in the developing countries, of the donor international development partners, such as the World Bank, the IMF and the other international NGOs, need to be seriously addresses if their intentions and efforts are not to be thwarted.

Sub-Saharan African countries would be most appreciative of the efforts of their development partners if due cognizance is given to their culture in the provision of assistance. Culture is to man as water is to fish. When fish is taken out of water for any reasonable time,it dies. Similarly African countries are so immersed in their culture that if the cultural perspectives are side-stepped in dealing with their developmental needs,nothing meaningful would be achieved .Since culture is the most powerful characteristic which defines the identity of a people,planning for any activity without the infusion of the core strategies of the culture of the people would be futile and subsequently fail.

Whatever assistance is given the developing recipient governments must be made to realize that, in view of the drastic and fast changes occurring all over the world because  of advanced technology in industry, transportation and communication these governments must take control over their own destinies since such a control is the essence of responsibility and is the most basic requirement for success. Solely relying on assistances from international donors and their strategies to solve the problems of the developing countries is not the realistic sustainable way .to improve the living standards of the people. The greatest power at their disposal is their ability to envision one's own fate ands to change accordingly. Personal commitment and the willingness to persevere are the guidelines for success and must begin with the recognition that change is necessary. Changing the ways things are done in these countries must start with a change in attitude and the governments must be stretched to reach the point where change almost comes unglued. It must be emphasized that without this change, these countries cannot compete in this fast track lane of development being pursued in the western industralised countries. They must either change or head for human extinction. For success to be achieved the governments of these countries must of necessity

1. control their own destinies and not let
   outsiders take over their destinies;
2. face the present realities of being in a highly competitive world

3. attempt to change the prevailing conditions
   before the situations compel them to do so.

The most important of the above conditions relates to "facing realities" .This is crucial in all aspects of life. Facing reality means dealing with what everybody would wish to avoid namely danger; failure; personal short-comings and others including serious illness. Recognizing the realities on the ground is the first step towards the needed change and this should be done by the governments themselves and not prompted by outsiders.

A reality that is presently in vogue is the globalization .Its effects are pervasive. Globalization is certainly a threat without rewards for the governments of the developing countries as they are constantly being made to overcome the "raising of the bar" syndrome.

In this book emphasis has been put on the issue of the deplorable living conditions in the developing countries south of the Sahara. The fact that these countries face preventable diseases, are very poor, have no adequate housing facilities, widening poverty and other conditions that can be controlled are enough pointers to the urgent need for changes .Science and technology do offer some scope of success if implemented taking into consideration of the culture and traditions of the people .

Development should not be seen in materialistic terms only. The spirituality of the people needs to be recognized and heralded It must be noted that it is not the number of high-tech domestic appliances, electronic gadgets and four wheel automobiles that should be the indexes of development in the developing countries .The ability of the citizens to be morally and spiritually sound that would produce disciplined societies is where these poor countries have their consolation. It is the disciplined and morally sound government that will see the need to provide the basic needs of its citizens. Provision of portable water is a priority, provision of quality education for the children, maintenance of good sanitation are all factors towards the eradication of the prevalent diseases like malaria, diarrheas, mental retardation among the children.

Application of science and technology policies that are locally designed would definitely help in the alleviation of these problems and help in the raising of the living standards of the people.

The tasks ahead are Herculean but not insurmountable if the African Union would spearhead the revival of the continental socio-economic development

# REFERENCES

"African Central To World Food Balance" In African
Farming And Food Processing, July/August 2006,
Alain Charles Publishing Ltd. London

"Common Infectious Diseases Worldwide" www.
factmonster.com/ipka/A09036.html

"Making the Most of Water Resources", Water Resources 2005.
In African Farming And Food Processing, July/August
2006, Alain Charles Publishing Ltd. London

"Nigeria's New Agenda" In African Farming And Food Processing,
July/August 2006, Alain Charles Publishing Ltd. London

Africa – Canada Forum and Canadian Council for International
Cooperation, 2002. The New Partnership for Africa's
Development (NEPAD): A Commentary, Ottawa. April 2002

Africa Malaria Report 2003: www.rbm.who.int/
amd2003/amr2003/chart.htm

Agricultural and Mineral Resources – African Countries
– World Reach/Exploring Africa http://exploringafrica.
matrix.msu.edu/teachers/curriculum/m6/natural

Aikenhead, G. S. (1996); Science Education: Border
        Crossing into the Sub-Culture of Science.
        Studies in Science Education, 27, 1-52

Aikenhead, G. S. (2001) Science Communication with the Public.
        In Susan M, Stocklmayer, Mishael M. Gore and Chris Bryant
        (Eds.) Science Communication in Theory and Practice.
        Kluwer Academic Publishers. Dordretcht, the Netherlands

Aikenhead, G. S. 91997); Towards A First Nation Cross-
        Cultural Science and Technology Curriculum.
        Science Education, 81, 217-238

Ajayi,S. I and Iyoha, M. A (1998) "Debt Overhang and
        Debt Forgiveness: The Case of the Severely-
        Indebted Low-Income Countries of Sub-Saharan
        Africa" *Journal Of Economic Management, Vol.5,*

Ajayi,S.I (2001) "What Africa Needs to do to Benefit from
        Globalization" *Finance and Development, Vol38 No.4 December*

Altieri, M. (2980); Agroecology: The Basis of Alternative
        Agriculture. Boulder, Co. Westview

Anamuah-Mensah, J. (2000); The Race Against Underdevelopment:
        A Mirage or Reality; Ghana Universities Press, Accra

Antobam, K. (1963) Ghana's Heritage of Culture;
        Koehler & Amelag, Leipzig

Anup Sha: (2005) Structural Adjustment – A Major Cause Of
        Poverty – Global Issues. http://www.globalissues.org

Archibald, J. 91995); Locally Developed Native Studies Curriculum:
        An Historical and Philosophical Rationale. In M.
        Battiste & J. Barman (Eds.). First Nations Education in

Canada: The Circle Unfolds (Page 288-312) Vancouver,
Canada: University Of British Columbia Press

Assimeng, M. (1981); Social Structures Of Ghana; Ghana
Publishing Corporation, Accra, Ghana

Atwater, M. M. (1996); Social Constructivism: Infusion into
the Multicultural Science Education Research Agenda.
Journal of Research in Science Teaching, 33, 821-837

Basala, G. (1967); The Spread of Western
Science. Science 156, 611-622

Benavote, A. (1992); Curricular Extent, Educational
Expansion and Economic Growth. Comparative
Educational Review, 36 (2); 150-174

Bertelsen, P. And Muller, J. (2001) Who are the Ignorant:
Current Transformations In Tanzanian Indigenous
Technology System. Paper for Nordic Africa
Days. The Nordic Africa Institute. Uppsale

Bilsel A And Oral, O.(1995) "Role Of Education, Science And
Technology In Developing Countries" *ASEE/IEEC
Frontiers In Education,95 Conference,Georgia Tech.*

Brea, J. "Why Natural Resources May Actually Hurt Poor Countries"

Brecher, J. (1999): Panic Rules: Everything You Want To Know
About The Global Economy, By Robin Hanhel

Broadhead, Lee-Anne (2002*)" International Environmental
Politics: The Link To Green Diplomacy" Boulder,
Lynn Reinner Publishers,2002*

Brokensha, D.; Warren, D. And Werner, O; (Eds) (1980);
     Indigenous Knowledge Systems and Development.
     Lanham MD: University Press of America

Bronowski, J. (1978); Magic Science and Civilization.
     Columbia University Press, New York

Brown-Acquaye H.A (2002), 'The Suame Magazine ' *in
     Mike Savage and Prem Naidoo (Eds.) Popularization of
     Science and Technology Education: Some Case Studies
     from Africa* ,Commonwealth Secretariat, London

Brown-Acquaye H.A. (2004) 'Prospects and Constraints
     for Science Education in Ghana' *Institute for African
     Development (AID)—Africa Notes, Cornell University, NY*

Brown-Acquaye, H.A (2001);" *Each is Necessary and None
     is Redundant: The Need for Science in Developing
     Countries*" Science Education,85,68-70

Bulac, A. (1995); Quoted In Irzik G. Philosophy Of Science
     And Radical Intellectual Islam In Turkey. In W. W.
     Cobern (Ed.) Social-Cultural Perspectives On Science
     Education: An International Dialogue. Kluwer
     Academic Publishers. Dordretcht, The Netherlands

Cajete, G. (1994); Look at the Mountain: Ecology of
     Indigenous Education. Colorado: Kivaki Press

Cervantes M and Gnellec D, (2002) "The Brain Drain:
     Old Myths, New Realities" *OECD Observer*

Chambers, D. W. (1983); Stereotypic Images of the Scientist: The
     Draw-A-Scientist Test. Science Education, 67, 255-265

Chambers, R.; Pacey, R. And Thrupp, L. (Eds.) (1989); Farmer First; Farmer Innovation and Agriculture Research. London: Intermediate Technology Publications

Choi H.S.(1988)" Science And Technology Policies In The Industrialization Of A Developing Country – Korean Approaches*" South Commission,1988 31 May, Geneva Switzerland*

Christie, M. J. (1991); Aboriginal Science for the Ecologically Sustainable Future. Australian Science Teachers Journal 37 (1) 26-31

CIA; The World Factbook (2002), Ghana

CIA; The World Factbook (2002), Malaysia

Cichocki, M. "The Aids Epidemic In Africa" File:// Cafe02/Shareddocs/Aidsinafrica.Htm

Cobern W. W. (1994); Cultural Constructivism: Approach to the Teaching of Evolution. SLCSP Working Paper No. 112

Cobern, W. W. (1988); Science and Social Constructivist View Of Science Education. In W. W. Cobern (Ed) Socio-Cultural Perspective on Science Education: An International Dialogue, Pg. 7-23. Kluwer Academic Publishers. Dordretcht, The Netherlands

Cobern, W. W. (1991) World View Theory and Science Education Research, NARST Monograph No. 3; Manhattan, K. S. National Association for Research in Science Teaching

Cobern, W. W. (1993) World View Theory and Science Education Research, NARST Monograph No. 3; Kansas State University, Manhattan, Kansas 66506

Cobern, W. W. (1993); Contextual Constructivism: The Impact of Culture on the Learning and Teaching Of Science. In K. G. Tobin (Ed.) Constructivists Perspective on Science and Mathematics Education. Washington DC. American Association for the Advancement of Science, Pg. 51-69

Cobern, W. W. (1994) World View, Culture and Science Education; Science Education International, Vol. 5 (4)

Cobern, W. W. (1996) Constructivism and Non-Western Science Education Research; International Journal of Science Education, 18, 295-310

Cobern, W. W. (2000) Everyday Thoughts about Nature; Kluwer Academic Publishers. Dordretcht, The Netherlands

Cohen, J. & Blanc, S. (1996); Girls In The Middle School: Working To Succeed In School. Washington DC. America Association of University Women Educational Foundation

Colgan, Ann-Louise (2002); Hazardous To Health: The World Bank And IMF In Africa; Africa Action, April 18, 2002

Collier, P. (2004) "Natural Resources and Conflict in Africa"http://www.crimesofwar.org/africa-,ag/afr_04_colhier.html.

Collision, C. O. Cited In Rollnick, M.; the Influence of Language In The Second Language Teaching And Learning Of Science. In W. W. Cobern (Ed.) Socio-Cultural Perspective on Science Education: An International Dialogue (1988) P. 121-137. Kluwer Academic Publishers, Dordretcht, the Netherlands

Common Infectious Diseases Worldwide. The Centers For Diseases Control (CDC); The World Health Organisation (WHO) http://factmonster.com/ipka/a090369.htm

Connor, S. Map of Epidemic Risk Areas in Africa. New York, International Research Institute for Climate Prediction. The Earth Institute At Columbia University, 2003 (http://edesnw4.cr.usgs.gov/adds)

Contreras, A. & Lee, O. (1990); Differential Treatment of Students By Middle School Science Teachings: Unintended Cultural Bias. Science Education 74 (4), 433-444

Coolier, P.And Gunning J. W.( 1998) "Explaining African Economic Performance" *Journal Of Economic Literature, 37,March*

Cooper, C; (1973); Science, Technology and Production in the Underdeveloped Countries An Introduction. In C. Cooper (Ed.) Science, Technology and Development Pg. 1-18. London, Frank Cass

Cox et al. Mapping Malaria Risk in the Highlands of Africa. London, MARA/London School of Hygiene and Tropical Medicine, 1999.

Cumminns, J. (1980); The Cross Lingual Dimensions Of Language Proficiency: Implications For Bilingual Education And The Optimal Age Issue. TESOL Quarterly 14: 175-187

Daily Graphic, April 24, 2007 – BBC Report; Daily Graphic Communications Group Ltd. Accra; Ghana

Daily Graphic, April 25, 2007 – BBC Report; Daily Graphic Communications Group Ltd. Accra; Ghana

Daily Graphic, April 27, 2007 – BBC Report; Daily Graphic Communications Group Ltd. Accra; Ghana

Daily Graphic, April 30, 2007 – BBC Report; Daily Graphic Communications Group Ltd. Accra; Ghana

Dart, F. E. (1972); Science And The Worldview.
Physics Today. 25(6) 48-54

Department Of Foreign Affairs, Republic of South Africa-
African Union In A Nutshell: Official Website
: http://www.dfa.gov.za/au_nutshell.htm

Department of Foreign Affairs, Republic of South Africa- Official
Website: http://www.dfa.gov.za/au.nepad/nepadbrief.htm

Devan J. And Tewari P. S (2001) "Brains Abroad"
*Mckinsey Quarterly No.4*

Dijksterhuis, E. J. (1986); The Mechanization Of
The World Picture: Pythagoras To Newton.
Princeton, NJ Princeton University Press

Driori, G. S. (1998); A Critical Appraisal Of Science Education
For Economic Development. In W. W. Cobern (Ed.)
Socio Cultural Perspectives In Science Education: An
International Dialogue. Pg. 49-74. Kluwer Academic
Publishers. Dordretcht. The Netherlands

Driver, R. & Bell, B.; Students Thinking And The
Learning Of Science. A Constructivist View.
School Science Review, March 443-456

Dudgeon, P. (1998) Valuing The Wisdom Of The Past. In L. Byrski
(Ed.) The Way Ahead Prominent Australian Talk About
The Future Of Our Nation. New Holland, Sydney

Fee, E. (1981); Feminism A Threat To Scientific Objectivity?
Journal Of College Science Teaching; XI (2), 84-92

Feyerabend, P. (1991) Preface To The Turkish Translation Of
Science In A Free Society. Translated By Amed Kardam,
Oozgur Bir Toplumda Bilim. Ayriviti Yayinevi; Istanbul

Fitznor, L. (1998), The Circle Of Life: Affirming Aboriginal
Philosophies In Everyday Living. In Mccance, DC (Ed.) Life
Ethics In World Religions. Atlanta, Georgia: Scholars Press

Fleer, M. (1997); Science, Technology And Culture: Supporting
Multiple Worldviews In Curriculum Design.
Australian Science Teachers Journal; 43(3) 13-18

Fortes (1954); A Demographic Field Study In Ashanti. Culture
And Human Fertility. UNESCO, 1954, 265

Fourez, G. (1988); Ideologies And Science Teaching. Bulletin
Of Science Technology And Society, 8, 269-277

Gallard, A. J. (1992); Creating A Multicultural
Learning Environment In Science Classrooms.
NARST NEWS 34 (14) 7-9

George Susan (1990), A Fate Worse Than Debt,
New York, Grove Weidenfeld, 1990

Ghandi, M. (1940); What Is Woman's Role? Harijan, 24

Glasersfeld, E. V. 91989); Cognition, Construction Of
Knowledge And Teaching. Synthese 80 (1) 121-140

Global Exchange, September 2001, How The International
Monetary Fund And The World Bank Undermine
Democracy And Erode Human Rights.

Glover, W. B. (1984); Biblical Origins Of Modern Secular Culture: An Essay In The Interpretation Of Western History. Macon GA Mercer University Press

Goduka, I. N. (1999); Affirming Unity-In-Diversity In South African Education: Healing With Ubunu. Cape Town: Juta

Good, R. & Schlagel, R. (1992); Contextual Realism In Science And Science Teaching. Paper Presented At The Second International Conference On The History And Philosophy Of Science And Science Teaching. Kingston, Ontario, Canada

Goodson, I. & Walker, R. (1989); Putting Life Into Educational Research. In R. R. Sherman & R. B. Webb (Eds.) Qualitative Research In Education: Focus And Methods. Philadelphia, PA. The Falmer Press

Gough, N. (1998); Al Around The World: Science Education, Constructivism And Globalization. Educational Policy, Vol. 12 (5), 507-524

Guimaraes, F. (1989) Technology Policy In Newly Industrial Countries: A Brazilian Perspective. Science And Public Policy, (16 (3); 167-175

Hanhel, R. (1999): Panic Rules, South End Press, 1999

Hanlon, J. And Pettifar, A. (2000); Kicking The Habit, Finding A Lasting Solution To Addictive Lending And Borrowing – And Its Corrupting Side-Effects, Jubilee Research, March 2000

Hay S. L. et al. Etiology of Inter-Epidemic Periods of Mosquito-Borne Disease. Proceedings Of The National Academy Of Sciences Of The USA, 2000, 97 (16) 9335-9339

Head, J. (1985); Personal Response To Science;
　　　　Cambridge University Press, Cambridge

Hewson, M. G. A. B. (1988). The Ecological Context Of Knowledge:
　　　　Implications For Learning Sciences In Developing
　　　　Countries. Journal Of Curriculum Studies. 20 (4)

Hodson, D. (1985); Philosophy Of Science, Science And Science
　　　　Education. Studies In Science Education, 12, 25-57

Hooykass, R. (1972); Religion And The Rise Of Modern Science.
　　　　Grand Rapids, ML Wm B. Eerdman's Publishing Co.

Horton, R. (1982); Learning And Teaching Science.
　　　　African Journal Of Science. Vol. 76, 397-403

Idowu, E. B. (1962); African Traditional
　　　　Religion. London: Longmans

Idrissou-Toure, A. (2005) Debt Cancellation: No Panacea
　　　　For Benin, Inter Press-Service, July 7, 2005

Inglis, R. (1993); An Investigation Of The Interrelationship In A
　　　　Second Language And The Understanding Of Scientific
　　　　Concepts. Proceedings Of The First Annual Meeting Of
　　　　The South African Association For Research In Mathematics
　　　　Education. Grahamston, South Africa, Rhodes University

Iyoha M (2003) "Impact Of Globalisation On Agricultural
　　　　Exports And Economic Development In Africa"
　　　　*Africa Notes Nov.-Dec. 2003. Institute For African
　　　　Development, Cornell University Ithaca NY*

Jalloh, B. (2007) "Africa: IMF. World Bank Are a Major
　　　　Cause of Poverty" Concord Times, Freetown.

Jambou R. Et Al. Malaria in the Highlands of Madagascar after Five Years of Indoor House Spraying Of DDT. Transaction of the Royal Society Of Tropical Medicine and Hygiene, 2001, 95 (1): 14-18

Jegede O (1994) "African Cultural Perspectives And The Teaching Of Science" Pp.120- 130 *In J. Solomon And G Aikenhead(Eds.) STS Education : International Perspectives On Reform .New York Teachers College Press.*

Jegede O. (1995); Collateral Learning And The Eco-Cultural Paradigm In Science And Mathematics Education In Africa. Studies In Science Education, 25, 97-137

Jegede, O. & Okebukola, P. A. (1991); The Effect Of Instruction On Socio-Cultural Beliefs Hindering The Learning Of Science. Journal Of Research In Science Teaching 28(3) 275-285

Josef De Beer (2002) "The NEPAD ROAD TO 2061 – Reflections On Science Education In South Africa – http://oumail.ou.edu/attach/aaas/programs.htm

Kamens, D. H. And Benavot, A. (1991); Elite Knowledge For The Masses: The Origins And Spread Of Mathematics And Science Education In National Curricular. America Journal Of Education, 99 (2), 237-180

Karenromp, E. L. Et Al "Malaria Attributable to the HIV-1 Epidemic, Sub-Saharan Africa – www.medscape.com/voewarticle/512027

Karugonjo, R. (2007) "Africa: Continent Riddled by Human Rights Violations" The Monitor, Kampala

Kearney, M. (1984) Worldview. Novaqto. CA Chandler And Sharp Publishers Inc.

Kearney, M. (1984); World View. Novato. DA, Chandler & Sharp Publishers Inc.

Keller, E. F. (1987); Women Scientist And Feminist Critiques Of Science. In S. Graubard (Ed), Daedalus, Learning About Women: Gender, Politics And Power Pp. 77-92; Cambridge MA, American Academy Of Sciences

Klein, N. (2005) "Africa's Natural Resource Wealth Should Benefit Africans – A Noose Not A Bracelet" http://www.progress.org/2005/africa05.htm

Knamiller G.(1989) "Linking School Science And Technology With School Science In Malawi" *Science Education Newsletter 84(1) 1-3*

Krashen, S. D. (1982); Principles And Practice In Second Language Acquisition. Oxford, UK Permagon Institute Of English

Kroma S (1995) "Indigenous Knowledge And Development " *IK Monitor 3 (3), December 1995*

Krugly-Smolska, E. (1995); Cultural Influences In Science Education. International Journal Of Science Education, 17 (1) 45-58

Kuada, J. & Chacha, Y. (1999); Ghana: Understanding The People And Their Culture. Woeli Publishing Services, Accra

Kuamah, T. (2002); Out-Dooring Of Babies – The North Ewe Example. Ammammresem; The Ghana Folklore Magazine, Vol. 1, Pg. 8, Accra

Kuamuah, T. (2002). Out Dooring Of Babies – The North Eve Example, AMMAMRESEM, Ghana Folklore Magazine Vol.1, Pg. 8

Kunnie, J. (1994); Models Of Black Theology: Issues
In Class, Culture And Gender, P. 41-42.
Pennsylvania: Trinity Press International

Laidlaw, K. (2001) Market Cure Proposed for Third World's Battered
Farmers, Gemini News Service, December 4, 2001.

Latour, B.; Science In Action. Cambridge, MA.
Harvard University Press

Layton, D.; Jenkins, E.; Macgill, S. & Darvey, A. (1993); Inarticulate
Science? Driffield, East Yorkshire, UK: Studies In Education

Lewin K.M. (2000) "Mapping Science Education Policy In
Developing Countries" *The World Bank Washington D.C.*

Lewis, K. M. (1993); Planning Policy On Science
Education In Developing Countries. International
Journal Of Science Education; 15 (1) 1-15

Linder, C. J. (1992); Is Teacher-Reflected Epistemology A Source
Of Conceptual Difficulty In Physics? International
Journal Of Science Education; 14 (1) 111-121

Lockwood, M. (2005); We Must Breed Tigers In
Africa, The Guardian, June 24, 2005

Lynas, M. (2000); Letter From Zambia, The
Nation, February 14, 2000

Maclvor, M. (1995); Redefining Science Education For Aboriginal
Students. In M. Batiste & J. Barman (Eds.). First Nation
Education In Canada: The Circle Unfolds (Pg 73-98).
Vancouver, Canada; University Of British Columbia Press

Madeley, John (1999): Big Business Poor Peoples;
    The Impact of Transnational Corporations
    on the World's Poor, Zed Books 1999

Malaria Epidemics and Their Control in Southern Africa.
    Epidemic Post Mortem for the 2000/2001
    Malaria Season. Harare, Southern African Malaria
    Control Programme (SAMC), 2002.

MARA/ARMA Collaboration, July 2002: www.mara.org.za

Marc Lee (2002) "Africa Shortchanged" Canadian Centre
    for Policy Alternatives, Vol. 4 (4), June 20, 2002

Mazrui, A. & Wagaw, T. (185); Towards Decolonizing
    Modernity: Education And Cultural Conflict In
    Eastern Africa. In The Educational Process And
    Historiography In Africa. Paris: UNESCO

Mbeki, T. (1999) African – The Time Has Come.
    Tafelberg Publishers Ltd. Cape Town

Mcmurty, J. (1998): Unequal Freedoms; The Global Market
    As An Ethical System; Kumarian Press, 1998

Museveni, Y. (1995); Does African Matter? New
    Perspectives Quarterly, 12 (4), 53

Naidoo, P., Savage, M. & Taole, K. (1998); Science Education
    And The Politics Of Equity. In W. W. Cobern (Ed);
    Socio-Cultural Perspectives On Science Education:
    An International Dialogue. Kluwer Academic
    Publishing. Dordretcht. The Netherlands

National Academy Of Sciences (1984); Science And Creationism: A View From The National Academy Of Sciences. Washington DC. National Academy Of Sciences

News From Africa (2003) "Mining Giant Fights Workplace HIV/AIDS

Ngwane G. (2003) "Africa's Development Problemantique – The Case of NEPAD" – Africa Notes, Nov. – Dec. 2003, Institute For African Development, Cornell University, Ithaca NY.

Nkrumah, K. (1965); Neo-Colonialism; The Last Stage Of Imperialism. New York International Publishers. New York

Nsana, B. (2001); Apprenticeship System And Entrepreneurial Skills Development – A Study Of Tanzanian And Rural And Urban Micro And Small Enterprises. Department Of Development And Planning. Aalborg University

Nyerere J. (1967) "Education For Self Reliance" *Dar Es Salaam. Government Press.*

Obadan M.J. (2001) *"African And The Challenge Of Globalisation: How Should The Continent Respond?"*

Obasanjo, O. (2000); Paper Delivered At The Final Plenary Session Of The World Education Forum, Dakar

OECD (2002) *"International Mobility Of The Highly Skilled"*

Ogawa, M. (1986); Towards A New Rationale Of Science Education In Non-Western Society. European Journal Of Science Education 8 (2) 113-119

Ogawa, M. (1995); Science Education In A Multi-Science Perspective. Science Education 79, 583-59319

Ogawa, M. (1998); A Cultural History Of Science Education In Japan. An Epic Description. In W. W. Cobern (Ed.) Socio-Cultural Perspectives On Science Education: An International Dialogue. P. 139-162. Kluwer Academic Publishers. Dordretcht, The Netherlands

Ogunniyi, M. B. (1983); Relative Effects Of A History/ Philosophy Of Science Course On Student Teachers' Performance On Two Models Of Science. Research In Science And Technological Education. 1 (2) 193-198

Ogunniyi, M. B. (1995); Race, Culture, Evolution And Traditional Worldviews: Challenges For Science Education In Africa. Inaugural Lecture, School Of Science And Mathematics Education, University Of The Western Cape, Bellville, South Africa

Ogunniyi, M. B.; Jegede, O.; Ogawa, M.; Yandila, D. C. & Oladele, F. K. (1995); Nature Of Worldview Presuppositions Among Science Teachers In Botswana, Indonesia, Japan, Nigeria And The Philippines. Journal Of Research In Science Teaching, 32, 817-831

Ogunsola L.A (2005) "Information And Communication Technologies And The Effects Of Globalosation: Twenty-First Century "Digital Slavery " For Developing Countries-Myth Or Reality?" *Electronic Journal Of Academic And Special Librarianship .Vol.6 No. 1-2*

Okeobukola, P. A. And  Jejede, O. J. (1988); Traditional Cosmology And Its Influence On Students' Acquisition Of Skills Of Scientific Observation. Paper Presented At The Annual Meeting Of The National Association For Research In Science Teaching. Lodge Of The Four Seasons. MO

Oman C. (1996) "Globalisation And Regionalisation In The
1980s And 1990s. *In Svetlicicim And Singer H.*

Osafo, K. "Nkrumah's Vision Live Son" Daily Graphic, April 27,
2007, Graphic Communications Group Ltd., Accra, Ghana

Our Common Future(1987) ; *The Brundtland Report, World
Commission On Environment And Development, UN New York.*

Ozel, I. (1992); Three Issues – Techne – Civilization
– Alienation. Cidam Yayinlarli: Istanbul

Patel, R. (2001) ; Comments on The Doha WTO
Conference, November 2001

Peacock A. (1995) "Access To Science Learning For
Children In Rural Africa" *International Journal
Of Science Education 17(12): 149-166*

Peat, D. (1994). Lighting The Seventh Fire.
New York: Carol Publishing

Peel, M. (2005) "Oil Resources Should Benefit All People"
Crimes of War Project 1994-2004. http://www.
crimesofwar.org/africa-,ag/afr_04_colhier.html

Phelan, P.; Davidson, A. & Cao, H. (1991); Students'
Multiple Worlds: Negotiating The Boundaries Of
Family, Peer And School Cultures. Anthropology
And Education Quarterly, 22 (3), 224-250

Pickering, A. (Ed) (1992); Science As Practice And Culture.
Chicago: University Of Chicago Press

Pomeroy, D. (1994); Science Education And Cultural Diversity:
Mapping The Field. Studies In Science Education 24, 49-73

Poole, H. E. (1968); The Effect Of Urbanization Upon Scientific Concept Attainment Among Hausa Children Of Northen Nigeria. British Journal Of Educational Psychology. 38, 57-63

Poole, M. W. (1998); Science And Science Education: A Judeo-Christian Perspective. In W. W. Cobern (Ed); Socio-Cultural Perspectives On Science Education: An International Dialogue. Kluwer Academic Publishing. Dordretcht. The Netherlands

1. Population And Development In Africa, OAU And ECA http://www.un.org/popin/iepd/pop/html

Posner, G. J; Strike, K. A; Hewson, P. W. And Gertzog, W. A. (1982). Accommodation Of Scientific Conception. Science Education 66 (20) 211-227

Posner, G. Strike, K.; Hewson, P. And Gertzog, W. (1982); Accommodation Of Scientific Conception: Toward A Theory Of Conceptual Change: Science Education: 66, 211-227

Prather, J. P. (1990); Tracing Science Teaching. Washington DC. National Science Teachers Association

Prevention and Control of Malaria Epidemics. Third Meeting of Technical Support Network, Geneva, World Health Organisation, 2002.

Prophet, B. and Dow, P. (1994); Mother Tongue Language and Concept Development in Science. Language, Culture and Curriculum. 7 (3), 205-216

Radhakrishnan, S. (1967) Religion in a Changing World. London, UK. George Allen & Unwin Ltd.

Ramanathan K.(1988) "Evaluating the National Science
and Technology Base :A Case Study in Sri
Lanka " *Science and Public Policy, 15 304*

Rich, A. (1979), On Lies, Secrets and Silence; Selected
Prose. 1966-1978. London: Norton

Richards, D. (1980); European Mythology: The Ideology of
Progress. In Asante, M. K. and Vandi, A. S. (Eds.);
Contemporary Black Thought: Alternative Analyses in Social
and Behavioural Sciences, P. 76-77. Beverly Hills: Sage

Robbins, R. (1999) Global Problems and the Culture
Of Capitalism, Allyn And Bacon

Rollnick, M. S. (1989); The Influence of Language on the
Second Language Teaching and Learning Science. In W.
W. Cobern (Ed.) Socio-Cultural Perspectives on Science
Education: An International Dialogue. P. 121-137. Kluwer
Academic Publishers. Dordretcht, The Netherlands

Rollnick, M. S; White, M. and Dison, L. (1992); Integration
Writing Skills into the Teaching of Chemistry; and
Easy Task With Bridging Students. Proceedings of the
Annual Conference of the South African Association for
Academic Development, Port Elizabeth, 3-5 December

Rosen S. Et Al (2004). The Cost Of HIV/AIDS to Businesses
in Southern Africa" AIDS 18: 317-324

Rostow, W. W. (1971); The Shapes of Economic Growth:
A Non-Communist Manifesto. Cambridge,
UK. Cambridge University Press

Rutherford, J. F. (1985); Lessons from Five Countries. In M.
S. Klein & J. F. Rutherford (Eds) Science Education

in Global Perspectives: Lessons from Five Countries.
P. 207-231, Boulder, Colo. Westview Press

Rutherford, M. (1993); Making Scientific Language Accessible to
Science Learners. Paper Presented at the First Annual Meeting
of the South African Association for Research in Mathematics
and Science (SAARMSE), Grahamston. South Africa

Sachs J and Shatz H (1994) "Trade And Jobs In US Manufacturing
"*Brookings Papers On Economic Activity 1,1994*

Sachs J. And Warner (1995) "Economic Reform and
the Progress of Global Integration" *Brookings
Papers on Economic Activity 1 (1995)*

Salam A. (1987) " Ideals and Realities" *Singapore:
World Scientific (1987)*

Salam A. (1988) "Notes On Science,Technology and Science
Education in the Development of the South." *The
Third World Academy of Sciences 1988, Trieste, Italy*

Sarpong, P. (1977); Girls' Nobility Rites in Ashanti. Ghana
Publishing Corporation, Tema, Ghana

Scantlebury, K. (1998); An Untold Story: Gender, Constructivism
and Science Education. In W. W. Cobern (Ed); Socio-
Cultural Perspectives on Science Education: An
International Dialogue, P. 99-120. Kluwer Academic
Publishing. Dordretcht. The Netherlands

Shah, Anup (2005) – Structural Adjustment- A Major Cause of
Poverty – www.globalissues.org/traderelated/sap.asp

Shishido T. (1983) "Japanese Industrial Development
and Policies for Science and Technology"
*Weekly Science .219, 21 January 1983*

Slattery, L. (1995); The Big Question? The Australian
Magazine, July 15-16, Page 12-19

Smith, J. W. (1994) The World's Wasted Wealth 2;
Institute For Economic Democracy

Smith, L. T. (1999); Decolonizing Methodologies. Research
and Indigenous People. Zed Books. London

Smolicz, J. J. And Nunan, E. E. (1975); The Philosophical
and Sociological Foundations of Science Education:
The Demythologizing of School Science.
Studies in Science Education, 2, 101-143

Solzhenitsyn, A. (1995). Cited In Cobern, W. W. Science And
Social Constructivist View Of Science Education. In W.
W. Cobern (Ed.) Socio-Cultural Perspectives On Science
Education: An International Dialogue. Pg. 7-23. Kluwer
Academic Publishers. Dordretcht, The Netherlands

Spindler, G. (1987); Education and Cultural Process: Anthropological
Approaches (2nd Ed.) Prospect Heights IL: Waveland Press

Stanley, W. B. & Brickhouse, N. W. (1994);
Multiculturalism, Universalism And Science
Education. Science Education, 78(4) 387-398

Stiglitz, J. (2000) What I Learned At The World Economic
Crisis. The Insider; The New Republic, April 17, 2000

Stiglitz, J. (2001); Interview With The Observer And
Guardian Newspaper, Uk, April 2001

Stiglitz, J. (2002); Globalization And Its
    Discontents, Penguin Books, 2002

Stiglitz, J. (2003), African Notes Feb.2003, Institute For African
    Development, Cornell University, Ithaca, New York

Stocklmayer, S. M. (2001); The Background to Effective
    Science Communication by the Public. In S. M.
    Stocklmayer, M. M. Gore and C. Bryant (Eds.); Science
    Communication in Theory and Practice (P.19) Kluwer
    Academic Publishing. Dordretcht. The Netherlands

Strevens, P. (1980); Teaching English as an International
    Language. Oxford. Permagon Press

Summers, L. (2000); Let Them Eat Pollution, The Economist,
    February 8, 1992. Quoted From Vandana Shiva,
    Stolen Harvest, South End Press, 2000

Sutherland, D. L. (1998); Aboriginal Students' Perception
    of the Nature of Science: The Influence of Culture,
    Language and Gender. Unpublished PhD Dissertation,
    University Of Nottingham, Nottingham, UK

Tan, C. (2002), Tackling The Commodity Price Should
    Be WSSD's Priority; TWN Briefings For WSSD,
    No. 14, Third World Network, August 2002

Tarnas, R. (1991); The Passion of the Western
    Mind. Ballantine Books. New York

Taylor, P. C.; & Cobern W. W. (1998); Towards A Critical Science
    Education. In W. W. Cobern (Ed); Socio-Cultural Perspectives
    on Science Education: An International Dialogue. Kluwer
    Academic Publishing. Dordretcht. The Netherlands

Tema, B. O. (2002); Science Education and Africa's Rebirth.
In C. A. Odora Hoppers (Ed.) Indigenous Knowledge
and Integration of Knowledge Systems. Towards
A Philosophy of Articulation. Pg. 128-140. New
Africa Books (Pty) Ltd. Clarement South Africa

Thabo Mbeki (2003). African Notes, May 2003, Institute for African
Development, Cornell University, Ithaca, New York.

The African Summit on Roll Back Malaria, Abuja, Nigeria, 25
April, 2000. Geneva, World Health Organization, 2000

The Impact of HIV & AIDS on Africa (2005) http://
www.avert.org/aidsimpact.htm

The New Partnership For Africa's Development (NEPAD) (2002)
The African Peer Review Mechanism (APRM) http://
www.au2002.gov.za/docs/summit_council/aprm.htm

The World Bank (2002) "Education And HIV/
AIDS: A Window Of Hope

Thelen, L. J. (1983); Values and Valuing Science.
Science Education, 67 92) 185-192

Tobin, K. (1990); Social Constructivist Perspectives on
the Reform of Science Education. The Australian
Science Teachers Journal, 36 (4), 29-35

Uka, E. M. (1991); Readings in African Traditional Religion,
Structure, Meaning, Relevance, Future. Bern: Peter Lang

Ul Haq. M (1996ed) *The Tobin Tax: Coping With Financial
Volatility" Oxford University Press 1996*

UNAIDS, 2006 Report On The Global AIDS Epidemic, Annex:
    HIV And AIDS Estimates And Data, 2005 And 2003

United Nations (2002) Coordinates 2002, Charting
    Progress Against AIDS, TB And Malaria,
    Geneva: UNICEF, UNAIDS And WHO

Wackerhausen (1999). Conference Paper. Ministry
    Of Education, Denmark. Pa

Watanabe, M. (1974); The Conception of Nature in
    Japanese Culture. Science, 188 (4122) 279-282

Watkins K. (1997) "Globalization and Liberalization:
    Implications for Poverty Distribution and Inequality"
    *UNDP Occasional Paper Washington DC*

Welch, C. (2000); Structural Adjustment Programs And
    Poverty Reduction Strategy: Foreign Policy In
    Focus, Vol. 5, November 14, April 2000

White Jr. L. (1967); The Historical Roots of our Ecological
    Crisis. Science, 155(3767) 1203-1207

World Bank (1993) *"Global Economic Prospects and the
    Developing Countries"* Washington DC

World Bank 2000 "Can Africa Claim the 21st. Century? *"World Bank
    1998 African Development Indicators 1998/99 Washington DC*

Worrall, E. The Burden of Malaria Epidemics and Cost-
    Effectiveness In Epidemic Situations In: Third MIM
    Pan-African Conference on Malaria, Arusha, Tanzania.
    17-22 November 2002. Bethsaida, MD Multilateral
    Initiative on Malaria: Annex II P. 367, Number 12.

Yager, R. E. (1991); The Constructivist-Learning
        Model: Towards Reform In Science Education.
        The Science Teacher, 58(6) 52-57

Young, M. F. D. (1976); The Schooling of Science. In G. Whittey
        and M. F. D. Young (Eds.) Explorations in the Politics
        of School Knowledge. Driffield. UK Nafferton Books

Ziman, J. (1999); Public Understanding of Science. Science,
        Technology and Human Values, 16(1), 99-105